MATH Trailblazers

A BALANCED MATHEMATICS PROGRAM INTEGRATING SCIENCE AND LANGUAGE ARTS

Unit Resource Guide
Unit 4
Place Value Concepts

THIRD EDITION

KENDALL/HUNT PUBLISHING COMPANY
4050 Westmark Drive   Dubuque, Iowa   52002

A TIMS® Curriculum
University of Illinois at Chicago

UIC The University of Illinois
at Chicago

The original edition was based on work supported by the National Science Foundation under grant
No. MDR 9050226 and the University of Illinois at Chicago. Any opinions, findings, and conclusions
or recommendations expressed in this publication are those of the author(s) and do not necessarily
reflect the views of the granting agencies.

1 2 3 4 5 6 7 8 9 10   11 10 09 08 07

Letter Home

Place Value Concepts

Date: _____

Dear Family Member:

For the next two weeks, your child will study place value—how to tell that the 1 in 15, for instance, has a value of ten whereas the 1 in 105 has a value of one hundred. We will be working with numbers through the thousands. This unit lays the groundwork for addition and subtraction of larger numbers, which we begin here but will study in more depth in several weeks.

We will use base-ten pieces to explore place value. Base-ten pieces, which are shown here, are blocks that come in groups of ones, tens, hundreds, and thousands. The values of different numbers become visible when they are shown using base-ten pieces.

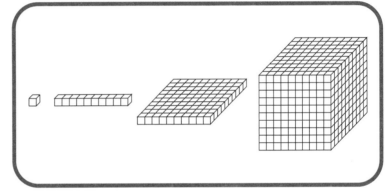

Base-ten pieces help children visualize a number's value.

You can provide additional math practice for your child at home.

- **Base-ten Shorthand.** Students will learn a simple way to record different numbers of base-ten pieces on paper. Ask your child to show you how to write some numbers between 1 and 9999 with this "base-ten shorthand."

- **Telling Time.** Your child will learn to tell time to the nearest five minutes. Ask your child to read a clock with hands at different times of the day.

- **Math Facts.** Help your child practice the subtraction facts in Groups 5 and 6 using flash cards.

Thank you for taking time to talk with your child about what he or she is doing in math.

Sincerely,

_____

Carta al hogar

Conceptos de valor posicional

Fecha: _____

Estimado miembro de familia:

Durante las próximas dos semanas, su hijo/a estudiará el valor posicional, es decir, cómo saber que el 1 en 15 tiene un valor de diez mientras que el 1 en 105 tiene un valor de cien. Trabajaremos con números hasta las unidades de mil. Esta unidad es la base para la suma y resta de números grandes, los cuales comenzaremos a estudiar a partir de ahora pero estudiaremos en profundidad dentro de algunas semanas.

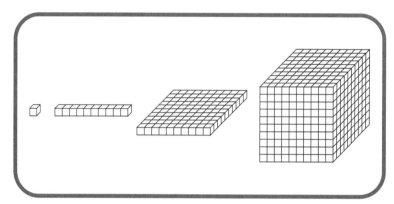

Usaremos piezas de base diez para explorar el valor posicional. Las piezas de base diez mostradas aquí son bloques que vienen en grupos de unidades, decenas, centenas y unidades de mil. Los valores de diferentes números resultan claros cuando se representan usando piezas de base diez.

Las piezas de base diez ayudan a los niños a visualizar el valor de un número.

Usted puede proporcionar práctica adicional para su hijo/a en casa.

- **Taquigrafía de base diez.** Los estudiantes aprenderán una forma sencilla de registrar distintos números de piezas de base diez en papel. Pídale a su hijo/a que le muestre cómo escribir algunos números entre el 1 y el 9999 usando esta "taquigrafía de base diez".
- **Decir la hora.** Su hijo/a aprenderá a decir la hora redondeando a los cinco minutos más cercanos. Pídale a su hijo/a que diga la hora en un reloj con manecillas a distintas horas del día.
- **Conceptos básicos.** Ayude a su hijo/a a practicar las restas básicas de los grupos 5 y 6 usando tarjetas.

Gracias por tomarse el tiempo para hablar con su hijo/a acerca de lo que está haciendo en la clase de matemáticas.

Atentamente,

_____

Table of Contents

Unit 4
Place Value Concepts

Unit 4

Outline
Place Value Concepts

Unit Summary

This unit extends students' work with place value to four-digit numbers and helps them build their understanding of our number system. The activities lay the conceptual groundwork for adding and subtracting four-digit numbers using paper-and-pencil procedures, which will be formally introduced in Unit 6. Base-ten pieces provide a concrete representation of the relationship between the different digits in our number system. They help students visualize how different digits in a number are used to represent different quantities. Students practice writing and telling time on analog and digital clocks. They continue to practice this skill in the Daily Practice and Problems and in future units. The DPP for this unit reviews the subtraction facts for Groups 5 and 6 and develops strategies for the multiplication facts for the twos and threes.

Major Concept Focus

- number sense
- partitioning numbers
- regrouping
- place value
- base-ten number system
- multidigit addition
- addition algorithms
- ordering large numbers
- telling time to five minutes
- Student Rubric: *Knowing*
- subtraction facts review for Groups 5 and 6
- multiplication facts strategies for the 2s and 3s

Pacing Suggestions

- Lesson 2 *The TIMS Candy Company* develops place value concepts using base-ten pieces. It takes three to five days to complete. Students' familiarity with base-ten pieces and place value concepts will govern how many sessions they need to complete the activities.

- Lesson 6 *Time for Problems* is a series of word problems appropriate to assign for homework. The lesson is also suitable for a substitute teacher since preparation is minimal.

Assessment Indicators

Use the following Assessment Indicators and the *Observational Assessment Record* that follows the Background section in this unit to assess students on key ideas.

A1. Can students partition large numbers into two and three parts and represent them with number sentences?

A2. Can students represent four-digit numbers using base-ten pieces, words, symbols, and place value charts?

A3. Can students read and write large numbers (to the thousands)?

A4. Can students compare and order large numbers (to the thousands)?

A5. Can students represent addition problems using base-ten pieces?

A6. Can students tell time to the nearest five minutes?

Unit Planner

	Lesson Information	Supplies	Copies/Transparencies
Lesson 1 **Breaking Numbers into Parts** URG Pages 23–38 DAB Pages 67–69 DPP A–D HP Parts 1–2 *Estimated Class Sessions* **2**	**Activity** Students partition two-digit numbers. They represent these groups with connecting cubes and discuss special groupings of tens and ones. **Math Facts** DPP Tasks B, C, and D develop strategies for the multiplication facts. **Homework** Assign Parts 1 and 2 of the Home Practice in the *Discovery Assignment Book.* **Assessment** Use the *Observational Assessment Record* to note students' abilities to partition and represent numbers using connecting cubes.	• 100 connecting cubes per student pair	• 3 copies of *Connecting Cubes Recording Sheet* URG Page 34 per student • 1 copy of *Base-Ten Board Part 1* URG Page 32 per student pair • 1 transparency of *Base-Ten Board Part 1* URG Page 32, optional • 1 transparency of *Connecting Cubes Recording Sheet* URG Page 34, optional • 1 copy of *Observational Assessment Record* URG Pages 11–12 to be used throughout this unit
Lesson 2 **The TIMS Candy Company** URG Pages 39–67 SG Pages 44–51 DAB Pages 71–74 DPP E–J *Estimated Class Sessions* **3-5**	**Activity** Students represent quantities with base-ten pieces. **Math Facts** DPP items E, F, G, and H provide practice with math facts. **Homework** 1. Assign *Questions 1–9* in the Homework section after Part 3. 2. Assign *Questions 10–12* in the Homework section after Part 4. 3. Students practice the subtraction facts in Group 5 using their flash cards. **Assessment** Students complete the *Are These the Fewest Possible?* and *Are They the Same?* Assessment Blackline Masters.	• 1 set of base-ten pieces (2 packs, 14 flats, 30 skinnies, and 50 bits) per student pair or group of 3 • 1 envelope per student for storing flash cards • tape, optional	• 1 copy of *Are These the Fewest Possible?* URG Page 56 per student • 1 copy of *Are They the Same?* URG Page 57 per student • 1 copy of *Base-Ten Board Part 1* and *Part 2* URG Pages 32–33 per student • 1 copy of *Base-Ten Recording Sheet* URG Page 58 per student or more as needed • 1 copy of *Base-Ten Pieces Masters* URG Pages 59–60 or more as needed, optional • 1 transparency of *Base-Ten Board Part 1* and *Part 2* URG Pages 32–33 • 1 transparency of *Base-Ten Recording Sheet* URG Page 58 • 1 transparency of *Base-Ten Pieces Masters* URG Pages 59–60, optional

	Lesson Information	Supplies	Copies/ Transparencies
Lesson 3 **Base-Ten Addition** URG Pages 68–79 SG Pages 52–53 DAB Pages 75–76 DPP K–N HP Parts 3–4 *Estimated Class Sessions* **2**	**Activity** Students use base-ten pieces to model two-digit addition with regrouping. A standard addition algorithm is introduced. **Math Facts** DPP Bits K and M provide practice with the subtraction facts in Group 6. **Homework** 1. Assign Part 4 of the Home Practice. 2. Students practice the subtraction facts in Group 6 using their flash cards. **Assessment** 1. Students solve a problem and are assessed with the Student Rubric: *Knowing*. 2. Use Home Practice Part 3 as a quiz.	• 1 set of base-ten pieces per student pair or group of 3 • 1 envelope per student for storing flash cards	• 1 copy of *Base-Ten Board Part 1* and *Part 2* URG Pages 32–33 per student • 1 copy of *Base-Ten Recording Sheet* URG Page 58 per student or more as needed • 1 transparency of *Base-Ten Board Part 1* and *Part 2* URG Pages 32–33 • 1 transparency of *Base-Ten Recording Sheet* URG Page 58
Lesson 4 **Bubble Sort** URG Pages 80–83 DPP O–P *Estimated Class Sessions* **1**	**Activity** Students arrange numbers in order. **Assessment** Use the *Observational Assessment Record* to note students' abilities to compare and order large numbers.	• 1 sheet of paper or index card per student	
Lesson 5 **It's Time** URG Pages 84–95 SG Pages 54–55 DAB Page 77 DPP Q–T *Estimated Class Sessions* **2**	**Activity** Students practice telling time to the nearest five minutes. Students tell and write time on analog and digital clocks. **Math Facts** DPP items S and T provide practice with math facts. **Homework** Assign some or all of the Lesson 6 problems. **Assessment** Students complete the *Time* Assessment Page.	• 1 brass fastener per student • analog demonstration clock • 1 pair of scissors per student	• 1 copy of *Time* URG Page 93 per student

(Continued)

	Lesson Information	Supplies	Copies/Transparencies
Lesson 6 **Time for Problems** URG Pages 96–100 SG Page 56 DPP U–V *Estimated Class Sessions* **1**	**Activity** Students solve word problems about time. **Homework** Assign some or all of the *Time for Problems* as homework. Assessment 1. Use DPP Bit U as an assessment. 2. Use the *Observational Assessment Record* to note students' abilities to tell time to the nearest five minutes. 3. Transfer appropriate documentation from the Unit 4 *Observational Assessment Record* to students' *Individual Assessment Record Sheets.*	• students' analog clocks from Lesson 5	• 1 copy of *Individual Assessment Record Sheet* TIG Assessment section per student, previously copied for use throughout the year

Preparing for Upcoming Lessons

Place eyedroppers in a learning center for students to explore prior to beginning Unit 5. You may want to introduce eyedroppers in a whole-class setting. You will need to purchase three different brands of paper towels for Unit 5.

Connections

A current list of literature and software connections is available at *www.mathtrailblazers.com*. You can also find information on connections in the *Teacher Implementation Guide* Literature List and Software List sections.

Literature Connections
Suggested Titles

- Hutchins, Pat. *Clocks and More Clocks.* Aladdin Library. Hong Kong, 1994. (Lesson 5)
- Murphy, Stuart J. *Earth Day–Hooray.* HarperCollins Publishers, New York, 2004.
- Owen, Claire. *Magic Squares and More.* ETA/Cuisenaire, Vernon Hills, IL, 2005.
- Pinczes, Elinor. *One Hundred Hungry Ants.* Houghton Mifflin Company, Boston, MA, 1993.
- Tang, Greg. *Math Appeal.* Scholastic Press, New York, 2003.
- Wells, Robert E. *How Do You Know What Time It Is?* Albert Whitman and Company, Morton Grove, IL, 2002.

Software Connections

- *Math Concepts One . . . Two . . . Three!* develops number sense through practice with estimation, rounding, ordering, comparing, and writing numbers.
- *Mighty Math Calculating Crew* poses short answer questions about number operations and money skills.
- *Money Challenge* provides practice with money.
- *National Library of Virtual Manipulatives* website (http://matti.usu.edu) allows students to work with manipulatives including base-ten pieces, the abacus, and many others.
- *Numbers Recovered* provides practice working with place value.
- *Penny Pot* provides practice with counting coins.
- *Ten Tricky Tiles* provides practice with number facts through engaging puzzles.
- *Tenth Network: Grouping and Place Value* provides practice grouping objects by 2s, 5s, and 10s.

Teaching All Math Trailblazers Students

Math Trailblazers® lessons are designed for students with a wide range of abilities. The lessons are flexible and do not require significant adaptation for diverse learning styles or academic levels. However, when needed, lessons can be tailored to allow students to engage their abilities to the greatest extent possible while building knowledge and skills.

To assist you in meeting the needs of all students in your classroom, this section contains information about some of the features in the curriculum that allow all students access to mathematics. For additional information, see the Teaching the *Math Trailblazers* Student: Meeting Individual Needs section in the *Teacher Implementation Guide.*

Differentiation Opportunities in this Unit

DPP Challenges

DPP Challenges are items from the Daily Practice and Problems that usually take more than fifteen minutes to complete. These problems are more thought-provoking and can be used to stretch students' problem-solving skills. The following lessons have a DPP Challenge in them:

- DPP Challenge H from Lesson 2 *The TIMS Candy Company*
- DPP Challenges L and N from Lesson 3 *Base-Ten Addition*
- DPP Challenge R from Lesson 5 *It's Time*
- DPP Challenge V from Lesson 6 *Time for Problems*

Background
Place Value Concepts

This unit extends students' work with place value to four-digit numbers and helps them build an understanding of our number system, the base-ten place value system. The activities in this unit lay the conceptual groundwork for performing multi-digit addition and subtraction. Two-digit addition is reviewed. Three- and four-digit addition and subtraction algorithms are developed in Unit 6.

In the initial activities, students snap together individual cubes to make groups of ten. The physical act of snapping cubes together helps them become familiar with the idea of trading with the base-ten pieces. Students use cubes to partition numbers, leading to the notion of special partitions—those corresponding to multiples of 10. These activities help students think about how numbers can be formed. Partitioning is revisited throughout the unit to further develop number sense.

Base-ten pieces are used extensively to provide a concrete representation of the relationship between a digit's position and its value. This helps students understand how different digits in a number are used to represent different quantities. Children often experience difficulty with the base-ten system because the value of a digit, e.g., 2, depends on its position in a number, e.g., 231, 321, and 312. These difficulties become apparent when children try to make sense of the standard addition and subtraction algorithms. Research shows that students who learn to add and subtract using base-ten pieces have a much greater understanding of place value than those who do not (Fuson and Briars, 1990).

The physical appearance of base-ten pieces is particularly well-suited for developing an understanding of the base-ten system (National Research Council, 2001). The ratios of the blocks' sizes are the same as the ratio of their corresponding values in the base-ten system. See the table in Figure 1. If the smallest block (1 cm $\times$ 1 cm $\times$ 1 cm cube) is taken as 1, the next block is ten of these smaller blocks molded together. The next larger block is 100 of the smallest blocks, and the largest block is a cube that is 1000 of the smallest blocks. In later years, base-ten pieces can be used to develop decimal concepts.

The relationship of the block sizes also makes base-ten pieces an ideal tool for ordering numbers. Children develop number sense for larger numbers while working with the base-ten pieces. They can see that one or two of the large blocks will have many more units than the same number of smaller blocks. They compare, order, say, and write large numbers to gain confidence and fluency in working with numbers.

Base-ten pieces are introduced in the context of the TIMS Candy Company that produces chocolate candies called Chocos. Each piece is given a nickname so students and teachers can refer to the concrete materials separately from the numbers. This eliminates confusion when you want to distinguish base-ten pieces from the written number they represent, e.g., three "skinnies" from three in the tens position. In addition, using nicknames allows the flexibility to change the values of different pieces when decimals are introduced. See Figure 1. For example, in Grade 4 Unit 10 the flat is used as one whole, the skinny as one-tenth, and the bit as one-hundredth.

Nickname	Physical Representation	Shorthand
bit	1 cm × 1 cm × 1 cm block	•
skinny	1 cm × 1 cm × 10 cm block	
flat	1 cm × 10 cm × 10 cm block	
pack	10 cm × 10 cm × 10 cm block	

Figure 1: *Base-ten pieces*

A shorthand for drawing the blocks is also illustrated in the table. The shorthand allows both teachers and students to sketch the pieces quickly on an overhead projector, board, or piece of paper. The shorthand is a symbolic representation of the base-ten pieces that aids the abstraction process. You may wish to introduce the shorthand earlier than it is presented in the lesson.

Working with base-ten pieces helps students visualize our number system's ten-for-one equivalencies. Each piece, once assigned a value, retains this value, regardless of where it is placed. The value of the piece is immediately known from its appearance. Although we can teach students to place the skinnies (tens) to the left of the bits (ones), they are still able to determine the value of each piece without paying attention to its position.

To maximize the connection between the blocks and written numbers, students work with *Base-Ten Boards* and *Base-Ten Recording Sheets*. The *Base-Ten Board* is a mat with column markings. Students place their base-ten pieces on the boards.

They learn that the bits (the smallest blocks) are always placed in the right-most column, just as in our number system the right-most digit is the ones digit. Students can be told that each type of block has its own home. The bits live in the bits column, the skinnies in the skinnies column, flats in the flats column, and packs in the packs column. This greatly aids in the understanding of regrouping.

The *Base-Ten Recording Sheet* is used to record numbers and helps bridge the concrete with the abstract. Like the *Base-Ten Board,* this sheet also uses column markers to separate different sized pieces. By recording, for example, 2 in the skinnies column, students begin to understand that this 2 is different from recording 2 in the bits column. This leads to developing the notion of the values of the places. By recording their work from the beginning, students find it easier to adjust to working solely with numbers. When students have formed the connection between the blocks and numbers, they can easily form a mental picture of the blocks when working abstract problems. By recalling the blocks, students can make sense of regrouping when adding and subtracting. Then, they can figure out for themselves the steps involved. Subsequently, they make fewer mistakes and regard mathematics as a subject that should and does make sense.

In addition to place value, students use the context of the TIMS Candy Company to practice writing and telling time on analog and digital clocks. They will continue to practice this skill in the Daily Practice and Problems and in future units.

Resources

- Fuson, Karen C., and Diane J. Briars. "Using a Base-Ten Blocks Learning/Teaching Approach for First and Second-Grade Place-Value and Multidigit Addition and Subtraction." *Journal for Research in Mathematics Education,* 21 (3), pp. 180–206, 1990.
- National Research Council. "Developing Proficiency with Whole Numbers." In *Adding It Up: Helping Children Learn Mathematics.* J. Kilpatrick, J. Swafford, and B. Findell, Eds., pp. 181–229. National Academy Press, Washington, DC, 2001.

Observational Assessment Record

(A1) Can students partition large numbers into two and three parts and represent them with number sentences?

(A2) Can students represent four-digit numbers using base-ten pieces, words, symbols, and place value charts?

(A3) Can students read and write large numbers (to the thousands)?

(A4) Can students compare and order large numbers (to the thousands)?

(A5) Can students represent addition problems using base-ten pieces?

(A6) Can students tell time to the nearest five minutes?

(A7) _____

Name	A1	A2	A3	A4	A5	A6	A7	Comments
1.								
2.								
3.								
4.								
5.								
6.								
7.								
8.								
9.								
10.								
11.								
12.								
13.								

Name	A1	A2	A3	A4	A5	A6	A7	Comments
14.								
15.								
16.								
17.								
18.								
19.								
20.								
21.								
22.								
23.								
24.								
25.								
26.								
27.								
28.								
29.								
30.								
31.								
32.								

Unit 4

Daily Practice and Problems
Place Value Concepts

A DPP Menu for Unit 4

Two Daily Practice and Problems (DPP) items are included for each class session listed in the Unit Outline. A scope and sequence chart for the DPP is in the *Teacher Implementation Guide*.

Icons in the Teacher Notes column designate the subject matter of each DPP item. The first item in each class session is always a Bit and the second is either a Task or Challenge. Each item falls into one or more of the categories listed below. A menu of the DPP items for Unit 4 follows.

N Number Sense	✖ Computation	○ Time	▱ Geometry
A, C, D, H–J, L O, U, V	A, E, N–P, R, S, V		
⁵⁷ Math Facts	$ Money	⚖ Measurement	▨ Data
B–H, K, M, S, T	L, N, Q, R		

Practicing the Subtraction Facts

DPP items in this unit provide review of the subtraction facts for Group 5 ($7 - 3, 7 - 5, 7 - 2, 11 - 2, 8 - 6, 5 - 3, 8 - 2, 4 - 2, 5 - 2$) and Group 6 ($6 - 4, 6 - 2, 13 - 5, 8 - 5, 8 - 3, 13 - 8, 12 - 8, 12 - 4, 12 - 3$). Students can solve facts in these groups by counting back, counting up, or thinking addition (reasoning from related addition facts).

DPP items G and M ask students to use flash cards to study these subtraction facts and update their *Subtraction Facts I Know* charts. *Subtraction Flash Cards: Groups 5* and *6* are in the *Discovery Assignment Book* following the Home Practice. See DPP items E, K, and S for practice with these facts.

Developing Strategies for the Multiplication Facts

DPP items in this unit develop strategies for the multiplication facts for the twos and threes. See DPP items B, C, D, F, and T for work with these facts.

For information on practicing and assessing subtraction facts in Grade 3, see the Lesson Guide for Unit 2 Lesson 7 *Assessing the Subtraction Facts.* For information on studying the multiplication facts in Grade 3, see the DPP Guide for Units 3 and 11. For a detailed explanation of our approach to learning and assessing the math facts in Grade 3, see the *Grade 3 Facts Resource Guide* and for information for Grades K–5, see the TIMS Tutor: *Math Facts* in the *Teacher Implementation Guide.*

 **Daily Practice and Problems**

Students may solve the items individually, in groups, or as a class. The items may also be assigned for homework. The DPPs are also available on the Teacher Resource CD.

Student Questions	Teacher Notes

 Subtraction: Counting Strategies

Do these problems in your head. Write only the answers.

1. $20 - 3 =$

2. $31 - 2 =$

3. $100 - 80 =$

4. $40 - 38 =$

5. $11 - 8 =$

6. $51 - 49 =$

7. Explain your strategy for solving Question 6.

TIMS Bit

Students can solve these problems in many ways. For example, to subtract $31 - 2$, begin with 31 and count back 2, "30, 29."

To subtract $40 - 38$, begin with 38 and count up 2, "39, 40." Let students describe their strategies and discuss the advantages and disadvantages of the different strategies.

1. 17   2. 29

3. 20   4. 2

5. 3   6. 2

7. Possible strategy: Count backwards from 51 to 49.

 Story Solving

Write a story and draw a picture about 3×8.

Write a number sentence about your picture.

TIMS Task

Answers will vary.

$3 \times 8 = 24$

$24 = 3 \times 8$

Calculator Counting with 2s and 3s

Work with a partner. One partner will count; the other will time how long the counting takes. Take turns.

A. Predict how long it will take to count by 2s to 30. Use a calculator to count by 2s to 60. Say the numbers quietly to yourself. How long did it take?

B. Predict how long it will take to count to 30 by 3s. Use a calculator to count by 3s to 30. Say the numbers quietly to yourself. How long did it take?

TIMS Bit

Pressing 2 + = = = = on a calculator with a constant function will cause the calculator to count by 2s. (Note: Some calculators may use different keystrokes.)

Discuss patterns students notice as they count or discuss predictions they made. Did they predict the time for counting by 3s using information from another time they counted?

 Guess My Number Puzzles

1. I am an even number. I am more than 5 and less than 10. I am not 6. Who am I?

2. I am an odd number. I am between 20 and 25. I am 3 times some number. Who am I?

TIMS Task

1. 8
2. 21

Subtraction: Counting Strategies

Do these problems in your head. Write only the answers.

1. 7 − 3 =
2. 11 − 2 =
3. 8 − 6 =
4. 7 − 5 =
5. 5 − 3 =
6. 8 − 2 =
7. 40 − 20 =
8. 70 − 20 =
9. 50 − 20 =
10. Explain your strategy for solving Question 6.

TIMS Bit

This Bit reviews the facts in Group 5. Ask students to describe strategies. Counting back and counting up are common strategies for solving these problems.

1. 4   2. 9   3. 2
4. 2   5. 2   6. 6
7. 20   8. 50   9. 30

10. Possible strategy: Thinking addition. 2 + 6 = 8, so 8 − 2 = 6. Note that these facts are related to 8 − 6 = 2 in Question 3.

 Story Solving

7 × 2 = ? Write a story and draw a picture about 7 × 2. Write a number sentence on your picture.

TIMS Task

Students may wish to share their stories with the class.

G **Subtraction Flash Cards: Group 5**

1. With a partner, sort the flash cards into three stacks: Facts I Know Quickly, Facts I Know Using a Strategy, and Facts I Need to Learn.

2. Update your *Subtraction Facts I Know* chart. Circle the facts you answered quickly. Underline those you knew by using a strategy. Do nothing to those you still need to learn.

TIMS Bit

Students cut out *Subtraction Flash Cards: Group 5.* The flash cards are located in the *Discovery Assignment Book* after the Home Practice. After students sort, they should update the *Subtraction Facts I Know* chart. Students take the cards for Group 5 home to practice with their families.

| Student Questions | Teacher Notes |

 Magic Square: Sum = 18

Complete the magic square using the numbers 2, 3, 4, 5, 6, 7, 8, 9, and 10. Each row, column, and diagonal must have a sum of 18.

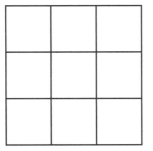

TIMS Challenge

One possible solution:

5	10	3
4	6	8
9	2	7

After students solve several magic squares, discuss patterns in the squares. Possible patterns: the number in the middle square is one-third the sum or the corner numbers are all odd and the middle number is even.

 Number of Students in School

How many students are in your school? Break this number into parts in at least three different ways. Write a number sentence for each way.

TIMS Bit

Encourage children to think in terms of hundreds, tens, and ones or to divide the number into equal parts. However, any correct grouping is fine. For example, if the number of students in a school is 462, then $400 + 60 + 2 = 462$ and $231 + 231 = 462$ are possible answers.

Number of Students in School Again

The number of students in your school is . . .

A. 10 more than ——

B. 10 less than ——

C. 100 more than ——

D. 100 less than ——

E. about half of ——

F. about twice ——

Choose another three-digit number. Complete the statements so they are true about the number you chose.

TIMS Task

After students write down their answers, let them discuss their strategies, as well as their answers, in groups or as a class.

 Subtraction: Thinking Addition

Do these problems in your head. Write only the answers.

1. 6 − 4 =   2. 6 − 2 =

3. 13 − 5 =   4. 8 − 5 =

5. 8 − 3 =   6. 13 − 8 =

7. 12 − 8 =   8. 12 − 4 =

9. 12 − 3 =

Update your *Subtraction Facts I Know* chart.

TIMS Bit

This Bit reviews the facts in Group 6. Students may use many strategies to find the answers. One useful strategy for this group is to "think addition." For example, knowing the addition fact $8 + 4 = 12$ can help solve $12 − 8 = 4$ and $12 − 4 = 8$. After students have written their answers, they can discuss the way they found the answers.

1. 2   2. 4

3. 8   4. 3

5. 5   6. 5

7. 4   8. 8

9. 9

$1000 to Share

Suppose you had nine $100 bills and two $50 bills.

1. How could you divide the money into two shares? Write a number sentence for each way. (The shares don't have to be equal.)

2. How could you divide the money into three shares? Write a number sentence for each way.

TIMS Challenge

Answers will vary. The total amount of money is $1000. As students write their number sentences, check to see that they are writing them correctly. Since 400 + 500 does not equal 1000, discourage students from writing number sentences like the following:

400 + 500 = 900 + 100 = 1000

Instead encourage them to write:

400 + 500 + 100 = 1000

 Subtraction Flash Cards: Group 6

1. With a partner, sort the flash cards into three stacks: Facts I Know Quickly, Facts I Know Using a Strategy, and Facts I Need to Learn.

2. Update your *Subtraction Facts I Know* chart. Circle the facts you answered quickly. Underline those you knew by using a strategy. Do nothing to those you still need to learn.

TIMS Bit

Students cut out *Subtraction Flash Cards: Group 6.* The flash cards are located in the *Discovery Assignment Book* after the Home Practice. After students sort, they should update the *Subtraction Facts I Know* chart. Have students take the cards for Groups 5 and 6 home to practice with their families.

Hot Dogs for Lunch

Fifteen Cub Scouts are planning an overnight camping trip. Two fathers will also go. They will have hot dogs for lunch.

1. If each scout eats two hot dogs and each father eats three hot dogs, how many hot dogs will they need?

2. Buns come in packages of 8 that cost $1 and hot dogs come in packages of 8 that cost $2. How much will all the buns and hot dogs cost?

TIMS Challenge

1. 36 hot dogs

2. $5 for buns
   $10 for hot dogs
   $15 total

 Boxes

How are these boxes alike?

```
1 ___ 2    4 ___ 5    10 ___ 11
|  10  |   |  22  |   |   46   |
4 ‾‾‾ 3    7 ‾‾‾ 6    13 ‾‾‾ 12
```

Make up two more boxes like these.

TIMS Bit

The number inside the box is the sum of the numbers on the corners. The numbers on the corners are consecutive numbers. Here is another example:

```
2 ___ 3
|  14  |
5 ‾‾‾ 4
```

P **Addition Practice**

Solve each problem in two ways. Use base-ten pieces, base-ten shorthand, or a short-cut method.

1. 65
   +35

2. 37
   +58

3. 49
   +22

TIMS Task ▨

Have base-ten pieces available. Methods will vary.

1. 100   2. 95   3. 71

Student Questions	Teacher Notes

 Coins

Marcus buys an apple for 45¢. He used 5 coins to pay for it. He didn't get any change back. What coins did he use?

Can you find more than one solution?

TIMS Bit $

One quarter and four nickels or four dimes and one nickel.

 Beans for Dinner

Fifteen Cub Scouts are planning an overnight camping trip. Two fathers will also go. They will have beans for dinner.

1. If three scouts share a can of beans and the two fathers share a can, how many cans of beans will they need?

2. If each can of beans costs 50¢, how much will the beans cost?

TIMS Challenge

Students may skip count as shown below:

1. 6 cans (3, 6, 9, 12, 15, 17)

2. $3.00 (50¢ + 50¢ + 50¢ + 50¢ + 50¢ + 50¢ = $3.00)

 More Subtraction

Do these problems in your head. Write only the answers.

1. 60 − 40 =   2. 60 − 20 =

3. 500 − 200 =   4. 80 − 60 =

5. 80 − 50 =   6. 80 − 30 =

7. 12 − 3 =   8. 120 − 30 =

9. 110 − 20 =

TIMS Bit

These problems use the facts from Groups 5 and 6. Students can skip count by tens to solve these problems.

1. 20   2. 40   3. 300
4. 20   5. 30   6. 50
7. 9   8. 90   9. 90

Story Solving

$3 \times 6 = ?$ Write a story and draw a picture about 3×6. Write a number sentence on your picture.

TIMS Task

Students may wish to share their stories with the class.

 More Boxes

What is special about these boxes?

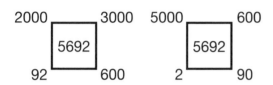

1. Make up another box for 5692.

2. Show 5692 using base-ten shorthand.

TIMS Bit

The number inside the box is the sum of the numbers on the corners. Making up these boxes provides more experience with partitioning.

1. Answers vary.

2. 5692

 Addition Squares

Fill in the boxes using the digits 1, 2, 3, and 4. Use each digit only once.

□ □ + □ □

1. What is the largest sum you can get?

2. What is the smallest sum you can get?

3. How many different sums can you find?

TIMS Challenge

The largest sum is $73 = 42 + 31$ or $73 = 41 + 32$. The smallest sum is $37 = 14 + 23$ or $24 + 13 = 37$.

There are 24 different addition problems that generate five different sums. The sums are 37, 46, 55, 64, and 73.

Lesson 1

Breaking Numbers into Parts

Lesson Overview

Estimated Class Sessions

2

Students review partitioning two-digit numbers into groups of their choice, representing them with connecting cubes and eventually discussing special groups of tens and ones. They then extend this work by partitioning three- and four-digit numbers.

Key Content

- Partitioning numbers in more than one way.
- Developing number sense for large numbers (to the thousands).
- Representing two-digit numbers using base-ten pieces.
- Understanding place value.

Key Vocabulary

- base-ten board
- bits
- digit
- Fewest Pieces Rule
- multidigit number
- partition
- recording sheet
- skinnies

Math Facts

DPP Tasks B, C, and D develop strategies for the multiplication facts.

Homework

Assign Parts 1 and 2 of the Home Practice in the *Discovery Assignment Book.*

Assessment

Use the *Observational Assessment Record* to note students' abilities to partition and represent numbers using connecting cubes.

Materials List

Supplies and Copies

Student	Teacher
Supplies for Each Student Pair	**Supplies**
• 100 connecting cubes	
Copies	**Copies/Transparencies**
• 3 copies of *Connecting Cubes Recording Sheet* per student (*Unit Resource Guide* Page 34) • 1 copy of *Base-Ten Board Part 1* per student pair (*Unit Resource Guide* Page 32)	• 1 transparency of *Base-Ten Board Part 1,* optional (*Unit Resource Guide* Page 32) • 1 transparency of *Connecting Cubes Recording Sheet,* optional (*Unit Resource Guide* Page 34) • 1 copy of *Observational Assessment Record* to be used throughout this unit (*Unit Resource Guide* Pages 11–12)

All blackline masters including assessment, transparency, and DPP masters are also on the Teacher Resource CD.

Student Books
Pack 'Em Up! (*Discovery Assignment Book* Pages 67–69)

Daily Practice and Problems and Home Practice
DPP items A–D (*Unit Resource Guide* Pages 14–15)
Home Practice Parts 1–2 (*Discovery Assignment Book* Page 60)

Note: Classrooms whose pacing differs significantly from the suggested pacing of the units should use the Math Facts Calendar in Section 4 of the *Facts Resource Guide* to ensure students receive the complete math facts program.

Assessment Tools
Observational Assessment Record (*Unit Resource Guide* Pages 11–12)

Daily Practice and Problems

Suggestions for using the DPPs are on page 30.

A. Bit: Subtraction: Counting Strategies (URG p. 14)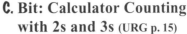

Do these problems in your head. Write only the answers.

1. $20 - 3 =$
2. $31 - 2 =$
3. $100 - 80 =$
4. $40 - 38 =$
5. $11 - 8 =$
6. $51 - 49 =$
7. Explain your strategy for solving Question 6.

C. Bit: Calculator Counting with 2s and 3s (URG p. 15)

Work with a partner. One partner will count; the other will time how long the counting takes. Take turns.

A. Predict how long it will take to count by 2s to 30. Use a calculator to count by 2s to 60. Say the numbers quietly to yourself. How long did it take?

B. Predict how long it will take to count to 30 by 3s. Use a calculator to count by 3s to 30. Say the numbers quietly to yourself. How long did it take?

B. Task: Story Solving (URG p. 14)

Write a story and draw a picture about 3×8.

Write a number sentence about your picture.

D. Task: Guess My Number Puzzles (URG p. 15)

1. I am an even number. I am more than 5 and less than 10. I am not 6. Who am I?
2. I am an odd number. I am between 20 and 25. I am 3 times some number. Who am I?

Before the Activity

You might laminate copies of the *Base-Ten Boards* Blackline Masters. Alternatively, use a long sheet of construction paper as base-ten boards since four columns fit reasonably well. Another alternative is simply to ask students to take out two sheets of paper and divide the paper into two columns. By placing them side-by-side, students have four columns for placing their base-ten pieces.

Students will need the *Base-Ten Board Part 1* to model two-digit numbers with the connecting cubes. The *Base-Ten Board Part 2* is used in later lessons.

Part 1 Partitions

Pass out connecting cubes. Write several two-digit numbers on a transparency or board, and ask students to think of two or three different ways to make each number with the cubes. For example, 12 might be represented with one group of 9 cubes and one group of 3 cubes; three groups of 4 cubes; or two groups of 5 cubes and one group of 2 cubes. This work will be familiar to students who have first- or second-grade experience with partitioning numbers.

Discuss different groupings or partitions for each of the numbers. During this discussion, write down students' suggestions using symbols, words, or pictures. Figure 2 shows some examples.

Stressing multiple representations—students' collections of cubes, verbal descriptions, words, symbols, and pictures—will help them see how different parts of each number make up the whole.

Guide the discussion so students see how some partitions are related to one another. For example, $9 + 9 + 9 + 9$, a representation of 36, can be regrouped by pairing the 9s to make $18 + 18$. Or $5 + 5 + 6$, a representation of 16, can be regrouped to make $10 + 6$.

Your discussion may lead to the idea that numbers can be partitioned into base-ten groups (ones, tens, hundreds, thousands, etc.). Students often do not require prompting to break numbers into tens and ones. They may notice that these groups correspond to the digits of the numbers. For example, two groups of ten and four ones correspond to the digits in 24. If, however, no student suggests breaking the number into tens and ones for any two-digit number, guide your students to think of ways to make the number using tens and ones. For instance, elicit the idea of grouping a number, such as 35, using tens and ones by asking:

- *The number 35 has a "3" and a "5." Is there a way to make 35 using 3 of some group and 5 of another group?*

Students need not master the base-ten groupings at this point. They will work with partitioning throughout the unit.

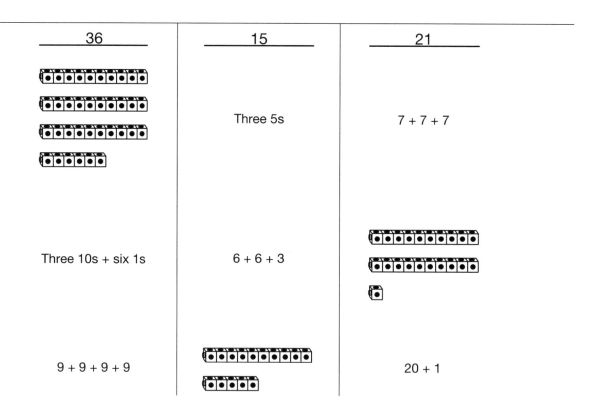

Figure 2: *Number groupings for 36, 15, and 21*

Once students have partitioned two-digit numbers and represented them with cubes, have them put the cubes away and partition numbers in their heads.

- *Partition 28, 49, and 60.*

Record these partitions on the overhead or board.

Ask the class to imagine they have as many connecting cubes as they could ever need. Ask:

- *How could you partition 123?*

If students have trouble partitioning 123, ask them how many cubes they would need to make 123. Then, ask them to break 123 into two parts or three parts. If needed, model partitioning 123 with cubes.

Continue with several other three-digit numbers; for example, 156, 230, or 407. Call special attention to base-ten groups as they occur. For example, 156 is $100 + 50 + 6$.

When children are comfortable with three-digit numbers, give them some four-digit numbers to partition; for example, 2134, 3409, or 4001. Some students may have difficulty imagining and working with such large numbers. Mastery is not essential at this point.

Part 2 Special Partitions

Pass out copies of the *Base-Ten Board Part 1, Connecting Cube Recording Sheet* Blackline Master, and connecting cubes. Explain to the class that they are going to help the TIMS Candy Company keep track of how many chocolate candies are produced. The candies are called Chocos. Each Choco is represented by a **bit** (an individual cube). Bits are always placed in the right-most column (the bits column) of the *Base-Ten Board Part 1*. Whenever there are ten bits, they can be packaged (snapped) together to make a **skinny.** Skinnies are always kept in the skinnies column. You can tell children that bits live in the bits column and skinnies in the skinnies column. (In this lesson, students make their own skinnies with connecting cubes. In subsequent lessons, they will use skinnies from the base-ten sets.)

Base-Ten Boards are used to emphasize the importance of columns and the relationships between the columns. For this lesson, students will only use Part 1, which has the bits and the skinnies. The other two columns will be introduced in the next lesson.

TIMS Tip

If you use the overhead projector for the connecting cubes, sketch the *Recording Sheet* on the board so children can see both simultaneously.

To help students make the connection between manipulatives and symbols, students record their work using numbers on the *Connecting Cubes Recording Sheet.* Refer to the Background for a more thorough discussion on the use of *Base-Ten Boards* and *Recording Sheets.*

Describe the following situation:

- *Eric works at the TIMS Candy Company. He made 12 Chocos and needs to keep track of his work.*
- *Count out 12 bits (connecting cubes) and place them in the bits column on the* Base-Ten Board.

Students should also record the number of bits on the *Recording Sheet* as demonstrated in Figure 3.

- *Can any of these bits be packed into a skinny? Remember, a skinny has 10 bits.*

Ten bits can be snapped together to form a skinny. Demonstrate snapping the cubes together. A skinny must be moved to the skinnies column. Two bits remain. Now record 1 skinny and 2 bits on the *Recording Sheet* as shown in Figure 4. Eric's work can be recorded as 12 bits or 1 skinny and 2 bits. Note to children the partition of 12 as 10 + 2.

- *Alissa also works at the TIMS Candy Company. She made 26 Chocos and needs to record her work.*
- *Count out 26 bits and place them in the bits column on the* Base-Ten Board.

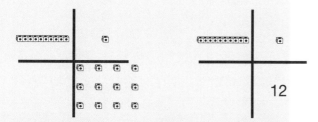

Figure 3: *12 bits represented on the* Base-Ten Board *and* Connecting Cubes Recording Sheet

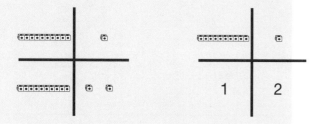

Figure 4: *1 skinny and 2 bits represented on the* Base-Ten Board *and* Connecting Cubes Recording Sheet

- *Can any of the bits be packed to make skinnies? How?* (The number 26 can be represented by 1 skinny and 16 bits or 2 skinnies and 6 bits.) Students record both ways on the *Connecting Cubes Recording Sheet* as shown in Figure 5.

Figure 5: *26 represented on the* Base-Ten Board *and* Connecting Cubes Recording Sheet

- *What partitions of 26 do you see?* (10 + 16 and 20 + 6)

Do several more examples such as 17, 23, or 35.

Explain to the class that the TIMS Candy Company likes to make as many skinnies as possible because it is hard to work with all the little bits. For example, the company likes to show 26 Chocos as 2 skinnies and 6 bits rather than 1 skinny and 16 bits or 26 bits. Since using 2 skinnies and 6 bits uses the fewest pieces, the company decided to call this the **Fewest Pieces Rule.** You may want to have the class count the number of pieces used in each representation (26 bits requires 26 pieces, 1 skinny and 16 bits is 17 pieces, 2 skinnies and 6 bits is 8 pieces).

- *What are all the different ways 32 can be shown on the* Base-Ten Board? *Record them on the* Connecting Cubes Recording Sheet. *Which way uses the Fewest Pieces Rule?*

Children should show all four ways (32 bits; 1 skinny and 22 bits; 2 skinnies and 12 bits; and 3 skinnies and 2 bits). They should recognize that 3 skinnies and 2 bits uses the fewest pieces. Note to students that they are finding special partitions—ones containing groups of 10, e.g., 10 + 22, 20 + 12, and 30 + 2.

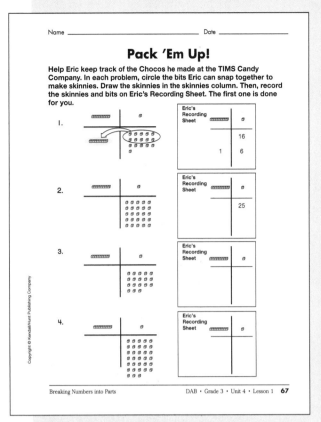

Discovery Assignment Book - page 67 (Answers on p. 36)

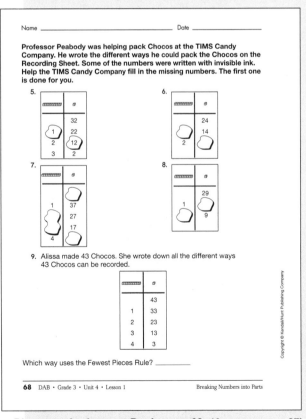

Discovery Assignment Book - page 68 (Answers on p. 37)

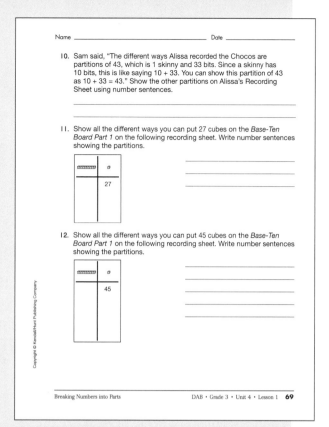

10. Sam said, "The different ways Alissa recorded the Chocos are partitions of 43, which is 1 skinny and 33 bits. Since a skinny has 10 bits, this is like saying 10 + 33. You can show this partition of 43 as 10 + 33 = 43." Show the other partitions on Alissa's Recording Sheet using number sentences.

_____
_____

11. Show all the different ways you can put 27 cubes on the *Base-Ten Board Part 1* on the following recording sheet. Write number sentences showing the partitions.

_____
_____
_____

12. Show all the different ways you can put 45 cubes on the *Base-Ten Board Part 1* on the following recording sheet. Write number sentences showing the partitions.

_____
_____
_____
_____
_____

Breaking Numbers into Parts   DAB • Grade 3 • Unit 4 • Lesson 1   **69**

Discovery Assignment Book - page 69 *(Answers on p. 38)*

Do several more of these as needed. If anyone observes that the Fewest Pieces Rule means using the digits in the number, bring this to everyone's attention. For example, when we write 23 bits using the Fewest Pieces Rule, we use 2 skinnies and 3 bits. Although these connections are obvious to adults, they often are not obvious to children.

Ask students to complete the *Pack 'Em Up!* Activity Pages in the *Discovery Assignment Book.*

Math Facts

DPP items B, C, and D develop strategies for the multiplication facts for the twos and threes.

Homework and Practice

- You may assign Parts 1 and 2 of the Home Practice in the *Discovery Assignment Book* as homework.

- DPP Bit A builds mental math skills using the counting-on and counting-back strategies to subtract.

Answers for Parts 1 and 2 of the Home Practice are in the Answer Key at the end of this lesson and at the end of this unit.

Assessment

Use the *Observational Assessment Record* to note students' abilities to partition and represent numbers using connecting cubes.

Unit 4 Home Practice

PART 1

1. A. 12 – 4 = _____
   B. 52 – 4 = _____
   C. 72 – 4 = _____

2. A. 3 + 8 = _____
   B. 43 + 8 = _____
   C. 123 + 8 = _____

3. Alicia's class has 34 students in it. Draw a picture to show how many teams of four can be formed. Write a number sentence to describe this problem.

4. A. Skip count by tens from 100 to 300.
   _____

   B. Skip count by hundreds from 100 to 1000.
   _____

PART 2

1. A. 80 – 20 = _____
   B. 30 + 40 = _____
   C. 50 – 30 = _____

2. A. 110 – 20 = _____
   B. 30 + 90 = _____
   C. 130 – 50 = _____

3. Break the following numbers into two, three, or four parts.
   A. 79 = _____ + _____
   B. 507 = _____ + _____
      507 = _____ + _____ + _____
   C. 1551 = _____ + _____ + _____
      1551 = _____ + _____ + _____ + _____

60 DAB • Grade 3 • Unit 4   PLACE VALUE CONCEPTS

Discovery Assignment Book - page 60 *(Answers on p. 35)*

At a Glance

Math Facts and Daily Practice and Problems

DPP items B, C, and D develop strategies for the multiplication facts. Bit A builds mental math and subtraction skills.

Part 1. Partitions

1. Students use connecting cubes to partition several two-digit numbers.
2. Discuss partitions, especially those involving multiples of ten.
3. Students partition numbers in their heads.
4. Students partition three-digit and four-digit numbers.

Part 2. Special Partitions

1. Introduce bits and skinnies and the columns on the *Base-Ten Board Part 1* using connecting cubes.
2. Model snapping 10 bits together to make a skinny.
3. Demonstrate using the *Connecting Cubes Recording Sheet*.
4. Practice regrouping various amounts and recording partitions on the *Connecting Cubes Recording Sheet*.
5. Note the partitions of hundreds, tens, and ones formed on the *Base-Ten Board Part 1*.
6. Introduce the Fewest Pieces Rule.
7. Students complete the *Pack 'Em Up!* Activity Pages in the *Discovery Assignment Book*.

Homework

Assign Parts 1 and 2 of the Home Practice in the *Discovery Assignment Book*.

Assessment

Use the *Observational Assessment Record* to note students' abilities to partition and represent numbers using connecting cubes.

Answer Key is on pages 35–38.

Notes:

Base-Ten Board Part 1

Skinnies

Bits

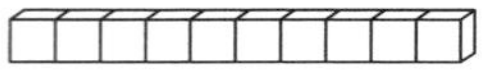

Blackline Master

Base-Ten Board Part 2

Flats

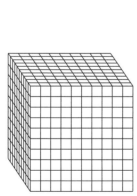

Packs

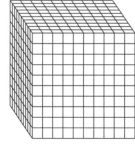

Connecting Cubes Recording Sheet

Discovery Assignment Book (p. 60)

Home Practice*

Part 1

1. **A.** 8
   B. 48
   C. 68

2. **A.** 11
   B. 51
   C. 131

3.

$\times\times$

$$8 \times 4 + 2 = 34$$

4. **A.** 100, 110, 120, 130, 140, 150, 160, 170, 180, 190, 200, 210, 220, 230, 240, 250, 260, 270, 280, 290, 300
   B. 100, 200, 300, 400, 500, 600, 700, 800, 900, 1000

Part 2

1. **A.** 60
   B. 70
   C. 20

2. **A.** 90
   B. 120
   C. 80

3. Answers will vary.
   A. 79 = 59 + 20
   B. 507 = 500 + 7
      507 = 100 + 400 + 7
   C. 1551 = 1000 + 500 + 51
      1551 = 1000 + 500 + 50 + 1

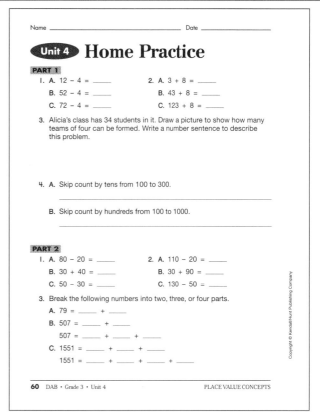

Name _____ Date _____

Unit 4 Home Practice

PART 1
1. **A.** 12 − 4 = _____   2. **A.** 3 + 8 = _____
   B. 52 − 4 = _____   **B.** 43 + 8 = _____
   C. 72 − 4 = _____   **C.** 123 + 8 = _____

3. Alicia's class has 34 students in it. Draw a picture to show how many teams of four can be formed. Write a number sentence to describe this problem.

4. **A.** Skip count by tens from 100 to 300.
   _____

   B. Skip count by hundreds from 100 to 1000.
   _____

PART 2
1. **A.** 80 − 20 = _____   2. **A.** 110 − 20 = _____
   B. 30 + 40 = _____   **B.** 30 + 90 = _____
   C. 50 − 30 = _____   **C.** 130 − 50 = _____

3. Break the following numbers into two, three, or four parts.
   A. 79 = _____ + _____
   B. 507 = _____ + _____
      507 = _____ + _____ + _____
   C. 1551 = _____ + _____ + _____
      1551 = _____ + _____ + _____ + _____

60 DAB • Grade 3 • Unit 4   PLACE VALUE CONCEPTS

Discovery Assignment Book - page 60

*Answers for all the Home Practice in the *Discovery Assignment Book* are at the end of the unit.

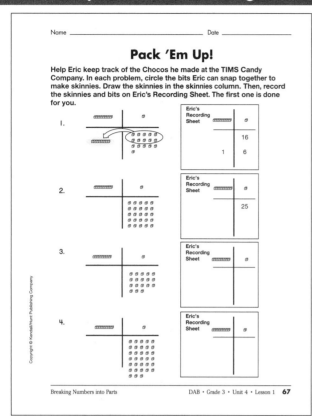

Discovery Assignment Book - page 67

Discovery Assignment Book (p. 67)

Pack 'Em Up!

1.

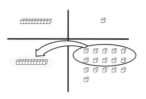

2.

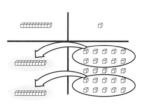

3.

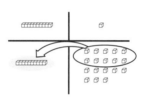

4.

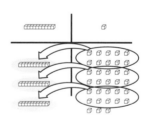

Discovery Assignment Book (p. 68)

5.

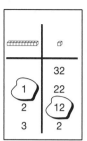

6.

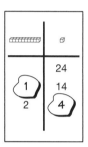

7.

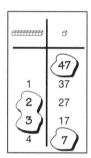

8.

9. The last one.

4 ▭▭▭ 3 ⬦

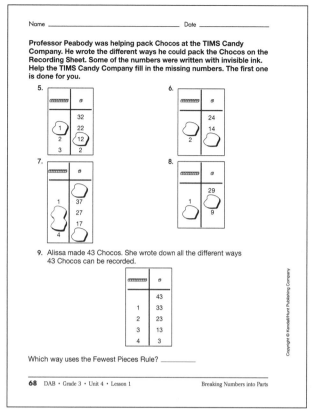

Discovery Assignment Book - page 68

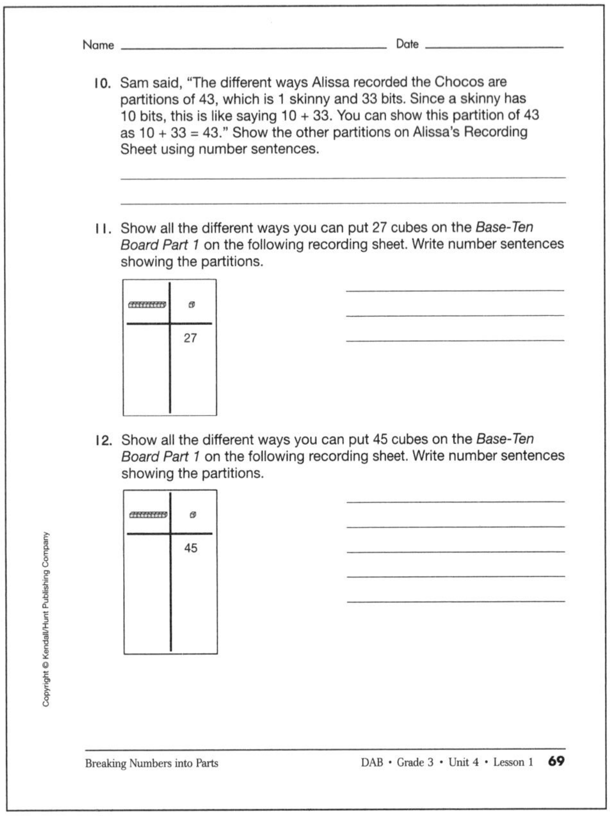

Name _____ Date _____

10. Sam said, "The different ways Alissa recorded the Chocos are partitions of 43, which is 1 skinny and 33 bits. Since a skinny has 10 bits, this is like saying 10 + 33. You can show this partition of 43 as 10 + 33 = 43." Show the other partitions on Alissa's Recording Sheet using number sentences.

_____
_____

11. Show all the different ways you can put 27 cubes on the *Base-Ten Board Part 1* on the following recording sheet. Write number sentences showing the partitions.

▭	▱
	27

_____
_____

12. Show all the different ways you can put 45 cubes on the *Base-Ten Board Part 1* on the following recording sheet. Write number sentences showing the partitions.

▭	▱
	45

_____
_____
_____
_____
_____

Copyright © Kendall/Hunt Publishing Company

Breaking Numbers into Parts   DAB • Grade 3 • Unit 4 • Lesson 1 **69**

Discovery Assignment Book - page 69

Discovery Assignment Book (p. 69)

10. $20 + 23 = 43$;

$30 + 13 = 43$;

$40 + 3 = 43$

11. $10 + 17 = 27$;

$20 + 7 = 27$

▭	▱
	27
1	17
2	7

12. $10 + 35 = 45$

$20 + 25 = 45$

$30 + 15 = 45$

$40 + 5 = 45$

▭	▱
	45
1	35
2	25
3	15
4	5

Lesson 2

The TIMS Candy Company

Estimated Class Sessions
3-5

This activity introduces base-ten pieces in the third grade. The context of the TIMS Candy Company is continued from the previous lesson. Students review rules for trading, practice ordering large numbers, and explore the hundreds and thousands places.

Key Content

- Understanding place value.
- Representing numbers using base-ten pieces and base-ten shorthand.
- Comparing and ordering large numbers.
- Partitioning numbers in more than one way.
- Writing numbers up to the thousands in words.

Key Vocabulary

- base-ten board
- bits
- flats
- packs
- recording sheet
- skinnies

Math Facts

DPP items E, F, G, and H provide practice with math facts.

Homework

1. Assign *Questions 1–9* in the Homework section after Part 3.
2. Assign *Questions 10–12* in the Homework section after Part 4.
3. Students practice the subtraction facts in Group 5 using their flash cards.

Assessment

Students complete the *Are These the Fewest Possible?* and *Are They the Same?* Assessment Blackline Masters.

Curriculum Sequence

Before This Unit

Students represented numbers using base-ten pieces in Grade 2 Unit 6. In Unit 11 they used the base-ten pieces to model subtraction of two-digit numbers requiring regrouping.

After This Unit

In Grade 3 Unit 6 students will use base-ten pieces to represent addition with three- and four-digit numbers. They will develop paper-and-pencil algorithms for addition and subtraction using the base-ten pieces.

Materials List

Supplies and Copies

Student	Teacher
Supplies for Each Student • 1 envelope for storing flash cards **Supplies for Each Student Pair or Group of Three** • 1 set of base-ten pieces: 2 packs, 14 flats, 30 skinnies (rods), and 50 bits (units) • tape, optional	**Supplies**
Copies • 1 copy of *Are These the Fewest Possible?* per student (*Unit Resource Guide* Page 56) • 1 copy of *Are They the Same?* per student (*Unit Resource Guide* Page 57) • 1 copy of *Base-Ten Board Part 1* and *Part 2* per student (*Unit Resource Guide* Pages 32–33) • 1 copy of *Base-Ten Recording Sheet* per student or more as needed (*Unit Resource Guide* Page 58) • 1 copy of *Base-Ten Pieces Masters* per student or more as needed, optional (*Unit Resource Guide* Pages 59–60)	**Copies/Transparencies** • 1 transparency of *Base-Ten Board Part 1* and *Part 2* (*Unit Resource Guide* Pages 32–33) • 1 transparency of *Base-Ten Recording Sheet* (*Unit Resource Guide* Page 58) • 1 transparency of *Base-Ten Pieces Masters,* optional (*Unit Resource Guide* Pages 59–60)

All blackline masters including assessment, transparency, and DPP masters are also on the Teacher Resource CD.

Student Books

The TIMS Candy Company (*Student Guide* Pages 44–51)
Subtraction Flash Cards: Group 5 (*Discovery Assignment Book* Pages 63–64)
The Company Pays Its Bills (*Discovery Assignment Book* Pages 71–72)
Getting To Know Base-Ten Shorthand (*Discovery Assignment Book* Pages 73–74)

Daily Practice and Problems and Home Practice

DPP items E–J (*Unit Resource Guide* Pages 16–18)

Note: Classrooms whose pacing differs significantly from the suggested pacing of the units should use the Math Facts Calendar in Section 4 of the *Facts Resource Guide* to ensure students receive the complete math facts program.

E. Bit: Subtraction: Counting Strategies (URG p. 16)

Do these problems in your head. Write only the answers.

1. $7 - 3 =$
2. $11 - 2 =$
3. $8 - 6 =$
4. $7 - 5 =$
5. $5 - 3 =$
6. $8 - 2 =$
7. $40 - 20 =$
8. $70 - 20 =$
9. $50 - 20 =$
10. Explain your strategy for solving Question 6.

F. Task: Story Solving (URG p. 16)

$7 \times 2 = ?$ Write a story and draw a picture about 7×2. Write a number sentence on your picture.

G. Bit: Subtraction Flash Cards: Group 5 (URG p. 16)

1. With a partner, sort the flash cards into three stacks: Facts I Know Quickly, Facts I Know Using a Strategy, and Facts I Need to Learn.
2. Update your *Subtraction Facts* I Know chart. Circle the facts you answered quickly. Underline those you knew by using a strategy. Do nothing to those you still need to learn.

H. Challenge: Magic Square: Sum = 18 (URG p. 17)

Complete the magic square using the numbers 2, 3, 4, 5, 6, 7, 8, 9, and 10. Each row, column, and diagonal must have a sum of 18.

I. Bit: Number of Students in School (URG p. 17)

How many students are in your school? Break this number into parts in at least three different ways. Write a number sentence for each way.

J. Task: Number of Students in School Again (URG p. 18)

The number of students in your school is . . .

A. 10 more than ___

B. 10 less than ___

C. 100 more than ___

D. 100 less than ___

E. about half of ___

F. about twice ___

Choose another three-digit number. Complete the statements so they are true about the number you chose.

Before the Activity

Use the *Base-Ten Pieces Masters* to model problems if base-ten pieces are not available. Copy the masters as necessary and ask students to cut out the models. You might copy the pieces onto heavy paper and attach magnetic tape to model problems on a magnetic board. The masters might also be used on the overhead if transparencies of the models are made.

Teaching the Activity

Part 1 Bits and Skinnies

Begin the lesson by reminding students of the TIMS Candy Company and how it needs to keep track of Chocos. This imaginary company is producing many more Chocos and needs to develop a more efficient set of blocks to keep track of them.

Pass out **bits** (1 cm × 1 cm × 1 cm blocks), **skinnies** (1 cm × 1 cm × 10 cm blocks), and copies of the *Base-Ten Board* and *Base-Ten Recording Sheet*. Tell students the bits will represent the individual Chocos, just as the connecting cubes did. The new set has a block to represent ten cubes already snapped together. Working with base-ten pieces differs from working with connecting cubes in that students must trade pieces instead of snapping cubes together. The first exercise repeats one in the previous lesson, with the important distinction that bits must be traded for skinnies. Explain that whenever students have ten bits, they can exchange them for one skinny.

Ask students to model problems with bits and skinnies as you call them out. For example

- *Eric made 24 Chocos. Show this amount by counting out 24 bits and placing them on the* Base-Ten Board Part 1.

Check that students have placed the bits in the bits column. Record this on a transparency of the *Base-Ten Recording Sheet.* Students should also record on their Recording Sheets.

- *Are there other ways to show twenty-four?*

At appropriate points during the lesson, you may wish to refer to bits as ones, skinnies as tens, flats as hundreds, and packs as thousands. Likewise, the bits column can be referred to as the ones column, and so on. However, when studying decimals in Grade 4, we will assign other values to the pieces. For example, to help students understand decimals, the flat can be the unit. Then the skinny is .1 (one-tenth) and the bit is .01 (one-hundredth).

Twenty-four bits can be shown as 1 skinny and 14 bits or as 2 skinnies and 4 bits. Model these amounts on the overhead. Demonstrate trading 10 bits for 1 skinny. Encourage students to record each model. See Figure 6.

	24
1	14
2	4

Figure 6: *Trading 10 bits for a skinny*

Call out other two-digit numbers and ask students to show them with their base-ten pieces. For example, place 5 skinnies and 6 bits on the overhead and ask students to show this amount in other ways. Observe students as they make trades and model different partitions of each number. Figure 7 shows six possible partitions of 56. Students can record them in any order, and it is not essential for every student to find all the partitions.

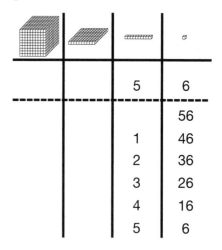

5	6
	56
1	46
2	36
3	26
4	16
5	6

Figure 7: *Partitions of 56*

Part 2 Flats and Packs
Flats. Pass out **flats** (1 cm × 10 cm × 10 cm blocks) and the *Base-Ten Board Part 2*. Explain that the TIMS Candy Company is growing and is producing more and more Chocos. The company decided that 10 skinnies should form a new group called a flat.

Place 10 skinnies side by side and show they are the same size as a flat. Ask students if they know how many bits are in a flat. Encourage them to find out.

Show the class 21 skinnies and ask:

* *How many flats can 21 skinnies make?*

Encourage students to use their *Base-Ten Board* and *Base-Ten Recording Sheet.* Students should see that they can form 2 flats with 1 skinny left over. Ask:

* *What number does this model represent?*

Students need to find out how many bits are in 2 flats and 1 skinny. There are 210 bits, thus the number represented is 210.

Repeat this exercise using different amounts. Stay with problems that require only one trade. Move on to problems that require more than one trade when students have had sufficient practice.

Sample problems include: 22 skinnies and 6 bits; 7 skinnies and 28 bits; 17 skinnies and 4 bits; 7 flats, 18 skinnies, and 19 bits.

Secret Numbers. Have students work in pairs modeling numbers. One partner picks a secret number and models it with base-ten pieces on the *Base-Ten Board.* The other person "decodes" the number by saying or writing it. Students should discuss what went wrong if they disagree on what the number is. Have students exchange roles and repeat this exercise.

Partitions and Regroupings. Show students 4 flats and ask:

* *How many skinnies will we have if we break up the 4 flats?* (Demonstrate the process of trading 10 skinnies for a flat. Students should observe that 4 flats have 40 skinnies.)
* *How many bits are in 40 skinnies?* (Since each skinny has 10 bits, they can skip count by tens to find that 40 skinnies have 400 bits.)

Show the class 1 flat, 2 skinnies, and 3 bits on the overhead. Write the amount in words—one hundred twenty-three. Ask students to tell and write how many bits are in the whole number. Students need to see, hear, and write numbers to become comfortable working with them. Add up the bits: $100 + 20 + 3 = 123$. Note that 1 flat, 2 skinnies, and 3 bits is a partition of 123. Encourage students to show other partitions of 123 bits, such as 12 skinnies and 3 bits, 11 skinnies and 13 bits, and 1 flat and 23 bits. Record these partitions on the *Base-Ten Recording Sheet.* Note that no matter how students group the pieces, 123 Chocos are still represented. Encourage students to find the partition that uses the Fewest Pieces Rule.

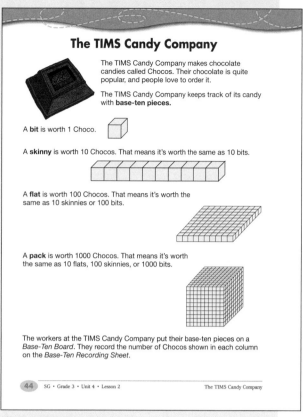

Student Guide - page 44

Explore other numbers by laying out different combinations of flats, skinnies, and bits and by asking your students to record them in various ways. Students may need additional practice writing, grouping, and partitioning numbers using the flats, skinnies, and bits before moving on to numbers involving packs. Students should work on their *Base-Ten Board* and with their *Base-Ten Recording Sheet* to represent partitions. Each time, encourage students to read the number and write it in words.

Provide additional examples as necessary. Here are some possible examples involving two trades:

- 3 flats, 18 skinnies, and 18 bits
- 2 flats, 15 skinnies, and 14 bits
- 1 flat, 10 skinnies, and 24 bits
- 0 flats, 20 skinnies, and 20 bits

Packs. Pass out **packs** (10 cm × 10 cm × 10 cm blocks). Explain that the TIMS Candy Company decided to sell large orders of Chocos in packs. Show how there are 10 flats in 1 pack. Challenge students:

- *Find out how many skinnies and bits are in a pack. Use your base-ten pieces. Explain your reasoning.* (There are 1000 bits in a pack and 100 skinnies in a pack.)

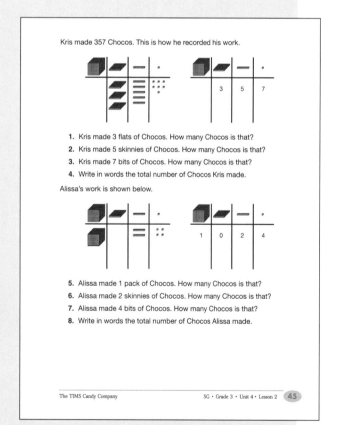

Student Guide - page 45 *(Answers on p. 61)*

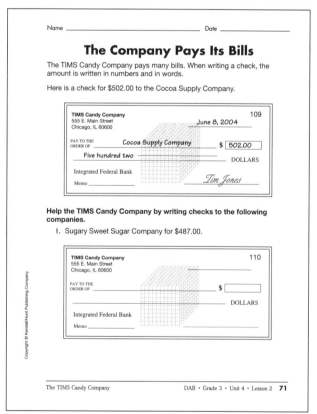

Discovery Assignment Book - page 71 *(Answers on p. 64)*

Discuss any patterns students may observe as they explore the base-ten pieces. Students should see that there are 10 bits in a skinny, 10 skinnies in a flat, and 10 flats in a pack. Instruct students to complete *Questions 1–14* on *The TIMS Candy Company* Activity Pages to reinforce their understanding of the pieces and their values.

For *Questions 9–14,* have students continue to work in pairs to model the numbers using base-ten pieces as they did for secret numbers. Partners take turns. One partner models the number and the other checks for accuracy.

Next, call out sample numbers such as those below: Have students place blocks including packs on their *Base-Ten Boards* and decide how many Chocos are represented.

- *1 pack, 3 flats, 2 skinnies, 5 bits* (1325 Chocos)
- *2 packs, 1 flat, 8 bits, 6 skinnies* (2168 Chocos)
- *3 skinnies, 1 pack, 4 flats* (1430 Chocos)
- *2 skinnies, 5 bits, 2 packs* (2025 Chocos)
- *1 pack, 3 flats* (1300 Chocos)

Have students place blocks including packs on the *Base-Ten Board* and decide how many Chocos are represented. The order in which the blocks are listed is purposefully mixed in some of the problems above. Students should observe that the value of a number is intrinsic in the block and does not depend on the order in which it is given. If your students are not ready for this, read the blocks in order from smallest to largest or largest to smallest. Ask students to write the number on the *Base-Ten Recording Sheet* and to also write the number in words. Read the numbers aloud.

Writing Numbers. Ask students to complete *The Company Pays Its Bills* Activity Pages in the *Discovery Assignment Book.* This will provide additional practice in writing numbers using words.

Repeat the Secret Number exercise in which one student picks a number and models it for another student to decode.

Name _____ Date _____

2. Recycled Paper Company for $105.00.

> **TIMS Candy Company** 111
> 555 E. Main Street
> Chicago, IL 60600
>
> PAY TO THE
> ORDER OF _____ $ [   ]
> _____ DOLLARS
>
> Integrated Federal Bank
> Memo _____

3. Box-It-Up Cardboard Company for $1006.00.

> **TIMS Candy Company** 112
> 555 E. Main Street
> Chicago, IL 60600
>
> PAY TO THE
> ORDER OF _____ $ [   ]
> _____ DOLLARS
>
> Integrated Federal Bank
> Memo _____

4. Bovine Dairy for $677.00.

> **TIMS Candy Company** 113
> 555 E. Main Street
> Chicago, IL 60600
>
> PAY TO THE
> ORDER OF _____ $ [   ]
> _____ DOLLARS
>
> Integrated Federal Bank
> Memo _____

72 DAB • Grade 3 • Unit 4 • Lesson 2   The TIMS Candy Company

Discovery Assignment Book - page 72 *(Answers on p. 65)*

Content Note

Usually when we write a number in the thousands, we do not use a comma to separate the thousands place. We write 3412. Numbers 10,000 and above usually include a comma after the thousands place. We write 32,412. The comma is a convention. It is not wrong to use a comma when writing a number in the thousands. Another convention that is becoming more and more common is to leave spaces between groups of numbers; for example, 23 345 176. Many European countries use the comma and period when writing numbers exactly opposite to the way we use them. A period is used between segments of a number larger than one and a comma marks off the decimal part of a number.

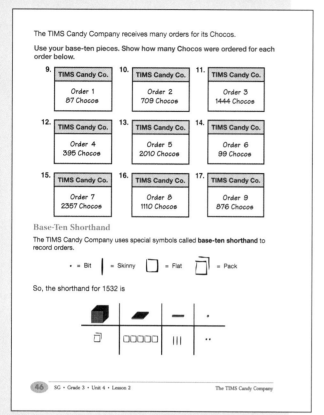

The TIMS Candy Company receives many orders for its Chocos.

Use your base-ten pieces. Show how many Chocos were ordered for each order below.

9.
TIMS Candy Co.
Order 1
87 Chocos

10.
TIMS Candy Co.
Order 2
709 Chocos

11.
TIMS Candy Co.
Order 3
1444 Chocos

12.
TIMS Candy Co.
Order 4
395 Chocos

13.
TIMS Candy Co.
Order 5
2010 Chocos

14.
TIMS Candy Co.
Order 6
99 Chocos

15.
TIMS Candy Co.
Order 7
2357 Chocos

16.
TIMS Candy Co.
Order 8
1110 Chocos

17.
TIMS Candy Co.
Order 9
876 Chocos

Base-Ten Shorthand

The TIMS Candy Company uses special symbols called **base-ten shorthand** to record orders.

• = Bit | = Skinny   ☐ = Flat   ⬚ = Pack

So, the shorthand for 1532 is

SG • Grade 3 • Unit 4 • Lesson 2   The TIMS Candy Company

Student Guide - page 46 (Answers on p. 61)

Introduce base-ten shorthand as a way of drawing the base-ten pieces. You can use the Base-Ten Shorthand section of *The TIMS Candy Company* Activity Pages to help introduce base-ten shorthand. Practice it with your students. Draw a number in shorthand as shown in Figure 8 and ask students what number it represents. Then ask students to use shorthand to represent certain numbers. Students may find it helpful to model a number with base-ten pieces first, then transcribe it into shorthand.

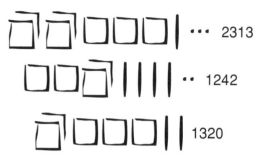

Figure 8: *Examples of shorthand numbers*

Now ask students to show several numbers and record them in base-ten shorthand; for example, 35, 167, 205, 354, 807, 1345, and 1003. Note that it is not necessary to draw the blocks in order. Assign *Questions 1–9* in the Homework section in the *Student Guide* after Part 3.

Part 4 The Fewest Pieces Rule

Remind students of the Fewest Pieces Rule discussed in Lesson 1 when working with the connecting cubes. This rule also applies when working with base-ten pieces. Model the rule with 14 skinnies. Ask:

- *Have I shown this number using the fewest pieces?* (No)

- *What should I trade to show this number following the Fewest Pieces Rule?* (Trade 10 skinnies for 1 flat.)

- *How do I show this number using the Fewest Pieces Rule?* (1 flat and 4 skinnies)

- *What number is this?* (140)

Repeat this series of questions, modeling with 24 skinnies and 14 bits. As you model with the base-ten pieces, also record the numbers on the transparency of the *Base-Ten Board* using base-ten shorthand. Record the trades as shown in Figure 9.

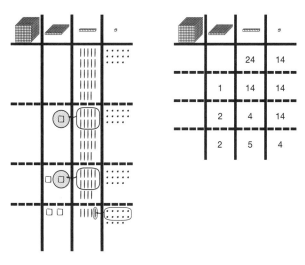

Figure 9: *Trading for the Fewest Pieces Rule and recording trades using base-ten shorthand*

Ask students to set base-ten pieces on their *Base-Ten Board* and then make trades according to the Fewest Pieces Rule. Suggest groupings of base-ten pieces, such as:

- *12 skinnies and 8 bits* (Trade 10 skinnies for one flat. 128 Chocos)
- *19 bits and 15 skinnies* (Trade 10 skinnies for one flat and 10 bits for 1 skinny. 169 Chocos)
- *11 flats, 3 skinnies, and 15 bits* (Trade 10 bits for 1 skinny and 10 flats for 1 pack. 1145 Chocos)
- *1 pack, 4 skinnies, 2 bits, and 13 flats* (Trade 10 flats for 1 pack. 2342 Chocos)
- *21 bits, 12 flats, and 13 skinnies* (See Figure 10.)
- *2 flats, 22 bits, 8 skinnies* (Trade 20 bits for 2 skinnies and 10 skinnies for 1 flat. 302 Chocos)
- *14 skinnies, 23 bits, 2 packs, and 1 flat* (2263 Chocos)

Make sure students are trading pieces correctly. Ask them to record their work on the *Base-Ten Recording Sheet* and write the amount of candy in words. If needed, they may say the blocks in order. Students' records should look similar to the sample, but the trading order can be different.

Note that the order of trading shown in Figure 10 is not right to left as is customary in the standard pencil-and-paper algorithm. It is natural for students to start with the largest block. To ease them into regrouping when adding and subtracting, you might suggest they start regrouping from the right.

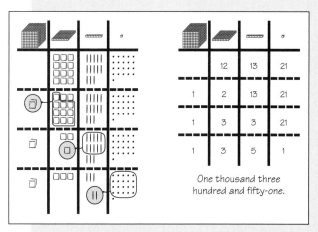

Figure 10: *Trading for the Fewest Pieces Rule*

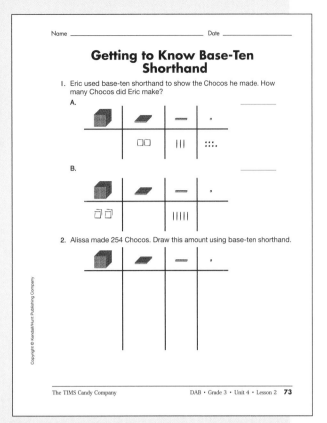

Discovery Assignment Book - page 73 (Answers on p. 65)

However, it is not incorrect to regroup from the left or to regroup in any other order. Have students complete the *Getting to Know Base-Ten Shorthand* Activity Pages in the *Discovery Assignment Book.*

Comparing and Ordering Numbers. Call out three numbers and have students model them with their base-ten pieces and arrange them in order. If students have difficulty with ordering, encourage them to compare two numbers at a time. For example, call out the numbers 1325, 2168, and 1300. Ask students which is larger, 1325 or 2168? Model both numbers with base-ten pieces. Students should explain that since packs contain the most candy, the 2168 must be larger. Compare 1325 and 1300. Since the number of packs is the same, students must look at the next smallest block, the flat. Because there are 3 flats in each, students must look at the skinnies. The first number has 2 skinnies and the second number has none, so the first number is the larger number. Continue with more examples as necessary. Instruct students to write the numbers in order, write them in words, and read them out loud. Lesson 4 *Bubble Sort* provides additional practice in ordering numbers.

Name _____ Date _____

3. Professor Peabody forgot to use the *Base-Ten Board* when he drew the Chocos he made at the TIMS Candy Company. Figure out how many Chocos Professor Peabody made.

A. _____

B. _____

4. Professor Peabody forgot to use the Fewest Pieces Rule to record his Chocos. Correct Professor Peabody's work by drawing the amount using the Fewest Pieces Rule. Write down how many Chocos were made.

A. _____

B. _____

C. _____

Discovery Assignment Book - page 74 (Answers on p. 66)

Up until now, students' work with the base-ten pieces has been on a *Base-Ten Board.* This emphasizes the importance of the columns and helps students keep track of their trading. Ask students whether they think they need to continue to use a *Base-Ten Board.* Students should realize that the type of block tells us its value. For example, if you hold up 2 flats, you have 200, 2 skinnies is 20, 2 packs is 2000, and 2 bits is 2. The order in which pieces are placed does not matter.

Encourage students to represent several numbers without a *Base-Ten Board.* For example, write the number 2357 on the board. Ask students to say the number. Then point to the 3 and ask them what the 3 means and to hold up blocks that represent the three. Students should hold up 3 flats and say that this is 300. Encourage them to identify the five, the two, and the seven. Students should see that 2357 is $2000 + 300 + 50 + 7$, a partition of the number 2357. Repeat with other four-digit numbers. Have students complete The Fewest Pieces Rule section in the *Student Guide.*

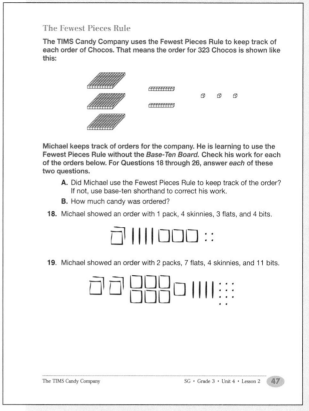

The Fewest Pieces Rule

The TIMS Candy Company uses the Fewest Pieces Rule to keep track of each order of Chocos. That means the order for 323 Chocos is shown like this:

Michael keeps track of orders for the company. He is learning to use the Fewest Pieces Rule without the *Base-Ten Board.* Check his work for each of the orders below. For Questions 18 through 26, answer *each* of these two questions.

   A. Did Michael use the Fewest Pieces Rule to keep track of the order? If not, use base-ten shorthand to correct his work.

   B. How much candy was ordered?

18. Michael showed an order with 1 pack, 4 skinnies, 3 flats, and 4 bits.

19. Michael showed an order with 2 packs, 7 flats, 4 skinnies, and 11 bits.

Student Guide - page 47 (Answers on p. 62)

20. Michael showed an order with 1 pack, 5 flats, 16 skinnies, and 3 bits.

21. Michael showed an order with 2 packs, 12 flats, 5 skinnies, and 4 bits.

22. Michael showed an order with 8 flats, 10 skinnies, and 5 bits.

23. Michael showed an order with 5 packs, 3 skinnies, and 7 bits.

24. Michael showed an order with 7 flats, 4 packs, and 7 bits.

Student Guide - page 48 (Answers on p. 62)

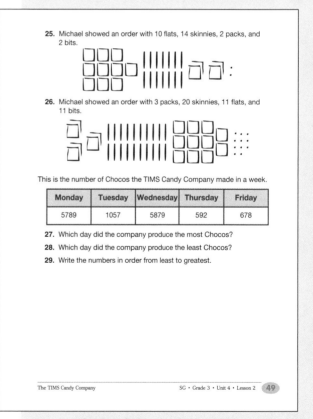

25. Michael showed an order with 10 flats, 14 skinnies, 2 packs, and 2 bits.

26. Michael showed an order with 3 packs, 20 skinnies, 11 flats, and 11 bits.

This is the number of Chocos the TIMS Candy Company made in a week.

Monday	Tuesday	Wednesday	Thursday	Friday
5789	1057	5879	592	678

27. Which day did the company produce the most Chocos?
28. Which day did the company produce the least Chocos?
29. Write the numbers in order from least to greatest.

Student Guide - page 49 (Answers on p. 63)

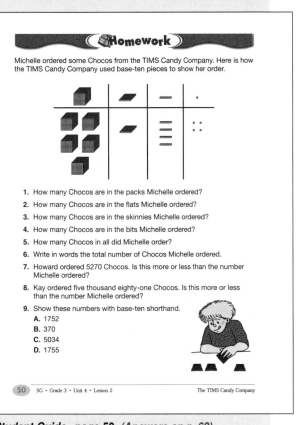

Student Guide - page 50 (Answers on p. 63)

Math Facts

DPP items E, F, G, and H provide practice with math facts. Bits E and G provide practice with the subtraction facts in Group 5. Task F asks students to illustrate a multiplication fact. Challenge H is a magic square.

Homework and Practice

- Assign **Questions 1–9** in the Homework section after Part 3.
- Assign **Questions 10–12** in the Homework section after Part 4.
- DPP items I and J build number sense. Bit I asks students to partition a number and Task J asks students to compare numbers.
- Remind students to take home their *Subtraction Flash Cards: Group 5* to practice with a family member.

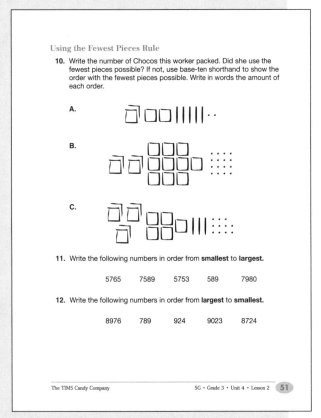

Student Guide - page 51 (Answers on p. 64)

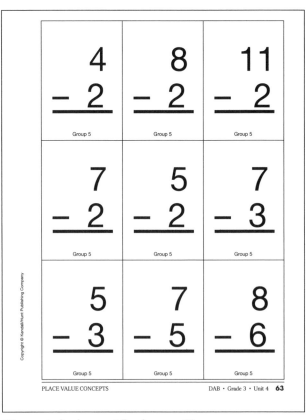

Discovery Assignment Book - page 63

Students complete the *Are These the Fewest Possible?* and *Are They the Same?* Assessment Blackline Masters. These pages will help you assess whether students are able to translate between different representations of multidigit numbers: base-ten pieces, base-ten shorthand, numbers, and words. They also assess whether students can implement the Fewest Pieces Rule.

At a Glance

Math Facts and Daily Practice and Problems

DPP items E, F, G, and H provide practice with math facts. Items I and J build number sense.

Part 1. Bits and Skinnies

1. Introduce bits and skinnies as a replacement for connecting cubes.
2. Students model two-digit numbers with base-ten pieces on their *Base-Ten Boards.*
3. Students learn to trade bits and skinnies.
4. Students identify partitions of numbers and record them on their *Base-Ten Recording Sheets.*

Part 2. Flats and Packs

1. Introduce flats and packs as a way to package larger orders of Chocos.
2. Students discuss the relationship between bits, skinnies, flats, and packs.
3. Student pairs take turns representing numbers with base-ten pieces and identifying the numbers.
4. Students represent partitions of three-digit numbers on their *Base-Ten Boards* and *Base-Ten Recording Sheets.*
5. Students complete *Questions 1–14* in *The TIMS Candy Company Activity Pages* in the *Student Guide.*
6. Students complete *The Company Pays Its Bills* Activity Pages.

Part 3. Base-Ten Shorthand

1. Students learn to represent base-ten pieces with base-ten shorthand.
2. Students answer *Questions 15–17* in the Base-Ten Shorthand section of *The TIMS Candy Company* Activity Pages in the *Student Guide.*
3. Students record partitions of numbers on their *Base-Ten Boards* using base-ten shorthand.

Part 4. The Fewest Pieces Rule

1. Remind students of the Fewest Pieces Rule discussed in Lesson 1.
2. Students represent numbers with base-ten pieces following the Fewest Pieces Rule.
3. Following the Fewest Pieces Rule, students record trades using base-ten shorthand on their *Base-Ten Boards.*
4. Students complete the *Getting to Know Base-Ten Shorthand* Activity Pages in the *Discovery Assignment Book.*
5. Students arrange numbers in order by comparing the largest base-ten pieces.
6. Students discuss representing numbers with base-ten pieces without using their *Base-Ten Boards.*
7. Students complete *Questions 18–29* in the Fewest Pieces Rule section of *The TIMS Candy Company* Activity Pages in the *Student Guide.*

At a Glance

1. Assign *Questions 1–9* in the Homework section after Part 3.
2. Assign *Questions 10–12* in the Homework section after Part 4.
3. Students practice the subtraction facts in Group 5 using their flash cards.

Assessment

Students complete the *Are These the Fewest Possible?* and *Are They the Same?* Assessment Blackline Masters.

Answer Key is on pages 61–67.

Notes:

Are These the Fewest Possible?

Janice is a new employee at the TIMS Candy Company. She needs some help learning how to use the Fewest Pieces Rule. Check each of her orders and figure out if she has done a good job.

1. 5 packs, 10 flats, 5 skinnies, 2 bits

    A. How many Chocos are in the order? _____

    B. Did Janice use the fewest pieces to keep track of the
order? _____
If not, use base-ten shorthand to show the fewest pieces possible.

2. 3 packs, 12 flats, 16 skinnies, 5 bits

    A. How many Chocos are in the order? _____

    B. Did Janice use the fewest pieces to keep track of the
order? _____
If not, use base-ten shorthand to show the fewest pieces possible.

3. 3 packs, 8 flats, 3 bits

    A. How many Chocos are in the order? _____

    B. Did Janice use the fewest pieces to keep track of the
order? _____
If not, use base-ten shorthand to show the fewest pieces possible.

Name _____   Date _____

Are They the Same?

There are different ways to show orders for Chocos. Questions 1–3 show a Chocos order slip and how a worker wrote the order with base-ten shorthand. Does the shorthand match the orders? If not, show the correct number of pieces with base-ten shorthand.

1.

TIMS Candy Co.
Order Slip 1 4212 Chocos

2.

TIMS Candy Co.
Order Slip 2 954 Chocos

3.

TIMS Candy Co.
Order Slip 3 4225 Chocos

Base-Ten Recording Sheet

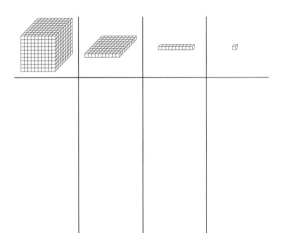

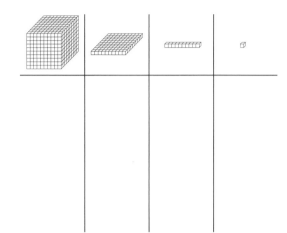

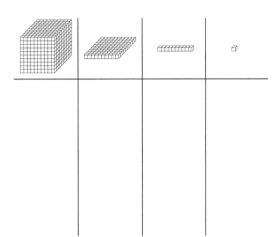

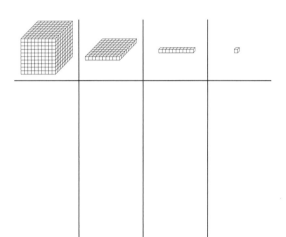

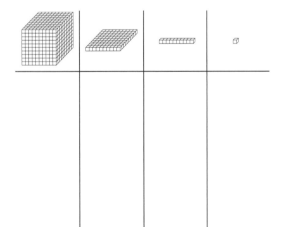

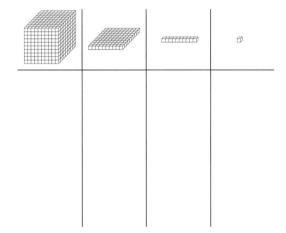

Base-Ten Pieces Masters

Base-Ten Pieces Masters

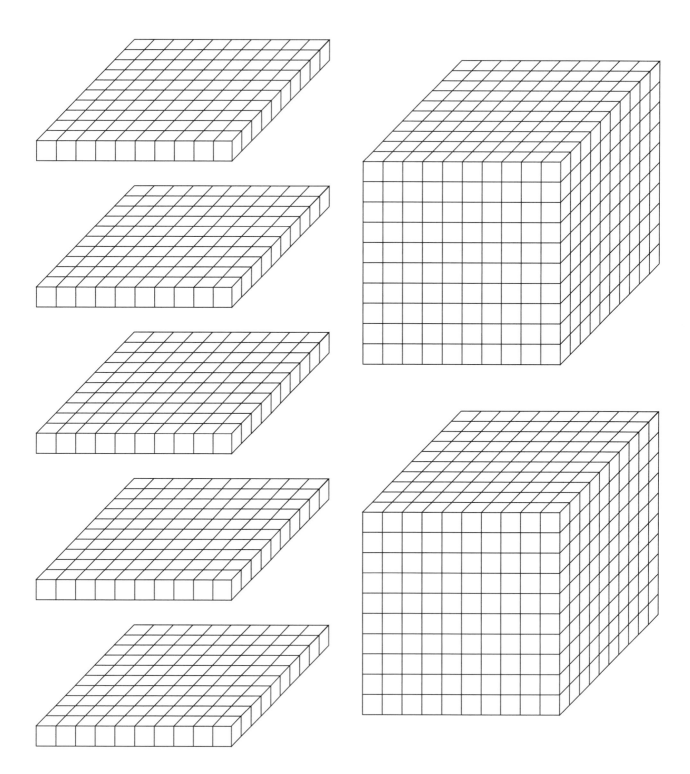

Student Guide (p. 45)

1. 300 Chocos
2. 50 Chocos
3. 7 Chocos
4. Three hundred fifty-seven Chocos
5. 1000 Chocos
6. 20 Chocos
7. 4 Chocos
8. One thousand twenty-four Chocos

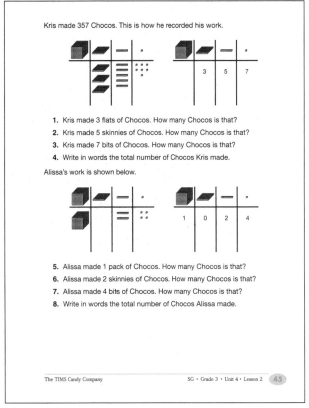

Student Guide - page 45

Student Guide (p. 46)

9. 8 skinnies, 7 bits
10. 7 flats, 9 bits
11. 1 pack, 4 flats, 4 skinnies, 4 bits
12. 3 flats, 9 skinnies, 5 bits
13. 2 packs, 1 skinny
14. 9 skinnies, 9 bits
15. 2 packs, 3 flats, 5 skinnies, 7 bits
16. 1 pack, 1 flat, 1 skinny
17. 8 flats, 7 skinnies, 6 bits

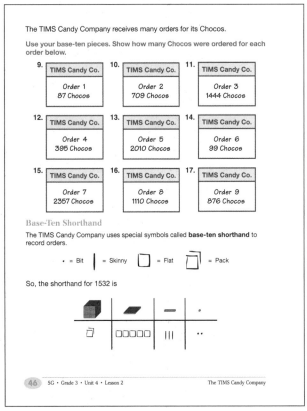

Student Guide - page 46

The Fewest Pieces Rule

The TIMS Candy Company uses the Fewest Pieces Rule to keep track of each order of Chocos. That means the order for 323 Chocos is shown like this:

Michael keeps track of orders for the company. He is learning to use the Fewest Pieces Rule without the *Base-Ten Board*. Check his work for each of the orders below. For Questions 18 through 26, answer *each* of these two questions.

A. Did Michael use the Fewest Pieces Rule to keep track of the order? If not, use base-ten shorthand to correct his work.

B. How much candy was ordered?

18. Michael showed an order with 1 pack, 4 skinnies, 3 flats, and 4 bits.

19. Michael showed an order with 2 packs, 7 flats, 4 skinnies, and 11 bits.

Student Guide - page 47

20. Michael showed an order with 1 pack, 5 flats, 16 skinnies, and 3 bits.

21. Michael showed an order with 2 packs, 12 flats, 5 skinnies, and 4 bits.

22. Michael showed an order with 8 flats, 10 skinnies, and 5 bits.

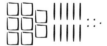

23. Michael showed an order with 5 packs, 3 skinnies, and 7 bits.

24. Michael showed an order with 7 flats, 4 packs, and 7 bits.

Student Guide - page 48

18. A. Yes
   B. 1344
19. A. No

   B. 2751

20. A. No

   B. 1663
21. A. No

   B. 3254
22. A. No

   B. 905
23. A. Yes
   B. 5037
24. A. Yes
   B. 4707

Student Guide (p. 49)

25. A. No

B. 3142

26. A. No

B. 4311

27. Wednesday

28. Thursday

29. 592, 678, 1057, 5789, 5879

25. Michael showed an order with 10 flats, 14 skinnies, 2 packs, and 2 bits.

26. Michael showed an order with 3 packs, 20 skinnies, 11 flats, and 11 bits.

This is the number of Chocos the TIMS Candy Company made in a week.

Monday	Tuesday	Wednesday	Thursday	Friday
5789	1057	5879	592	678

27. Which day did the company produce the most Chocos?

28. Which day did the company produce the least Chocos?

29. Write the numbers in order from least to greatest.

The TIMS Candy Company   SG • Grade 3 • Unit 4 • Lesson 2   49

Student Guide - page 49

Student Guide (p. 50)

Homework

1. 5000 Chocos

2. 100 Chocos

3. 40 Chocos

4. 4 Chocos

5. 5144 Chocos

6. Five thousand one hundred forty-four Chocos

7. more

8. less

9. **A.**

B.

C.

D.

Michelle ordered some Chocos from the TIMS Candy Company. Here is how the TIMS Candy Company used base-ten pieces to show her order.

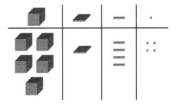

1. How many Chocos are in the packs Michelle ordered?

2. How many Chocos are in the flats Michelle ordered?

3. How many Chocos are in the skinnies Michelle ordered?

4. How many Chocos are in the bits Michelle ordered?

5. How many Chocos in all did Michelle order?

6. Write in words the total number of Chocos Michelle ordered.

7. Howard ordered 5270 Chocos. Is this more or less than the number Michelle ordered?

8. Kay ordered five thousand eighty-one Chocos. Is this more or less than the number Michelle ordered?

9. Show these numbers with base-ten shorthand.
   A. 1752
   B. 370
   C. 5034
   D. 1755

50   SG • Grade 3 • Unit 4 • Lesson 2   The TIMS Candy Company

Student Guide - page 50

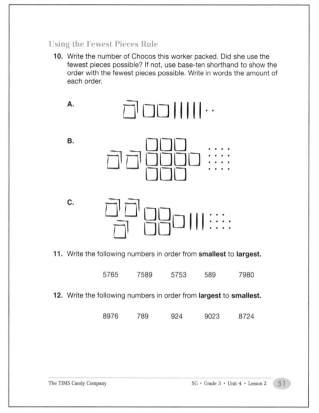

Using the Fewest Pieces Rule

10. Write the number of Chocos this worker packed. Did she use the fewest pieces possible? If not, use base-ten shorthand to show the order with the fewest pieces possible. Write in words the amount of each order.

A.

B.

C.

11. Write the following numbers in order from **smallest** to **largest**.

5765   7589   5753   589   7980

12. Write the following numbers in order from **largest** to **smallest**.

8976   789   924   9023   8724

The TIMS Candy Company   SG • Grade 3 • Unit 4 • Lesson 2   51

Student Guide - page 51

Student Guide (p. 51)

10. **A.** 1252; yes, one thousand two hundred fifty-two

    B. 3016; no, three thousand sixteen

    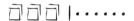

    C. 3541; no, three thousand five hundred forty-one

11. 589, 5753, 5765, 7589, 7980

12. 9023, 8976, 8724, 924, 789

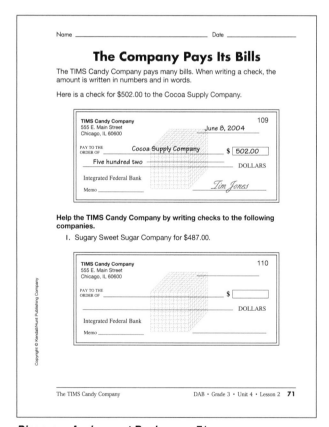

Name _____ Date _____

The Company Pays Its Bills

The TIMS Candy Company pays many bills. When writing a check, the amount is written in numbers and in words.

Here is a check for $502.00 to the Cocoa Supply Company.

TIMS Candy Company   109
555 E. Main Street
Chicago, IL 60600   June 8, 2004

PAY TO THE
ORDER OF ___ Cocoa Supply Company ___ $ 502.00

___ Five hundred two ___ DOLLARS

Integrated Federal Bank

Memo _____   Tim Jones

Help the TIMS Candy Company by writing checks to the following companies.

1. Sugary Sweet Sugar Company for $487.00.

TIMS Candy Company   110
555 E. Main Street
Chicago, IL 60600

PAY TO THE
ORDER OF _____ $ [   ]

_____ DOLLARS

Integrated Federal Bank

Memo _____   _____

The TIMS Candy Company   DAB • Grade 3 • Unit 4 • Lesson 2   **71**

Discovery Assignment Book - page 71

Discovery Assignment Book (p. 71)

The Company Pays Its Bills

1. Four hundred eighty-seven

Discovery Assignment Book (p. 72)

2. One hundred five

3. One thousand six

4. Six hundred seventy-seven

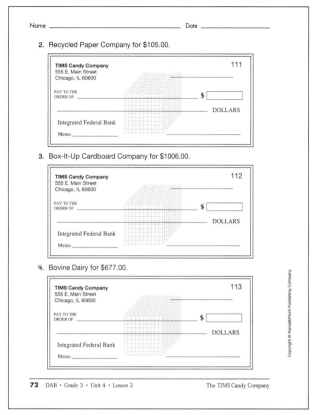

Discovery Assignment Book - page 72

Discovery Assignment Book (p. 73)

Getting to Know Base-Ten Shorthand

I. A. 237

B. 2050

2. □□ ||||| • • • •

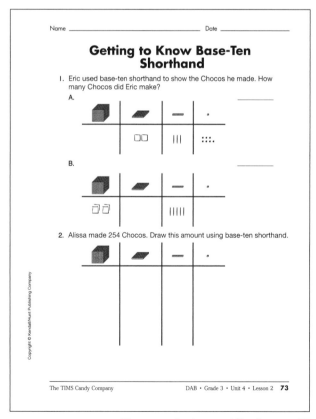

Discovery Assignment Book - page 73

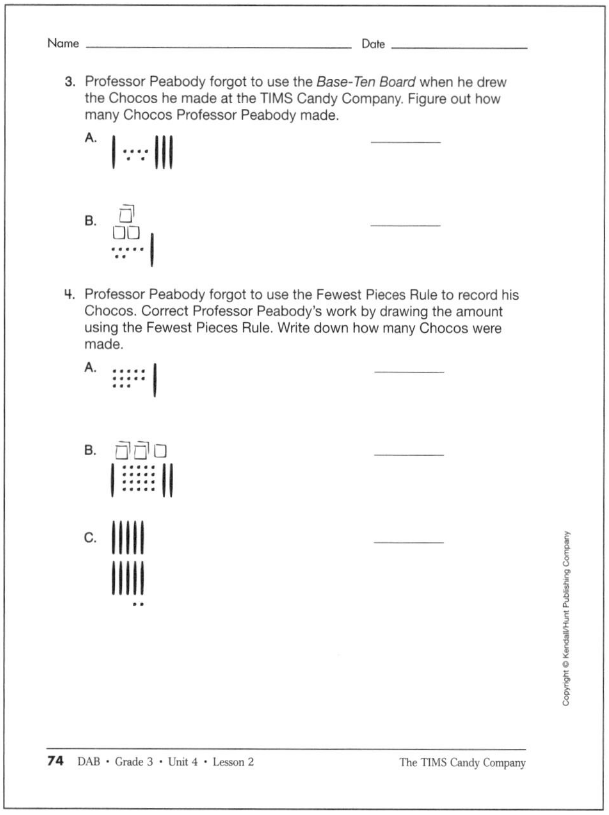

Name ______________ Date ______________

3. Professor Peabody forgot to use the *Base-Ten Board* when he drew the Chocos he made at the TIMS Candy Company. Figure out how many Chocos Professor Peabody made.

A. ______

B. ______

4. Professor Peabody forgot to use the Fewest Pieces Rule to record his Chocos. Correct Professor Peabody's work by drawing the amount using the Fewest Pieces Rule. Write down how many Chocos were made.

A. ______

B. ______

C. ______

Copyright © Kendall/Hunt Publishing Company

74 DAB • Grade 3 • Unit 4 • Lesson 2 The TIMS Candy Company

***Discovery Assignment Book* - page 74**

Discovery Assignment Book (p. 74)

3. **A.** 46

   B. 1217

4. **A.** 23

   B. 2150

   C. 102

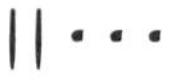

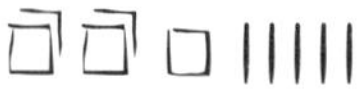

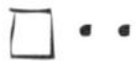

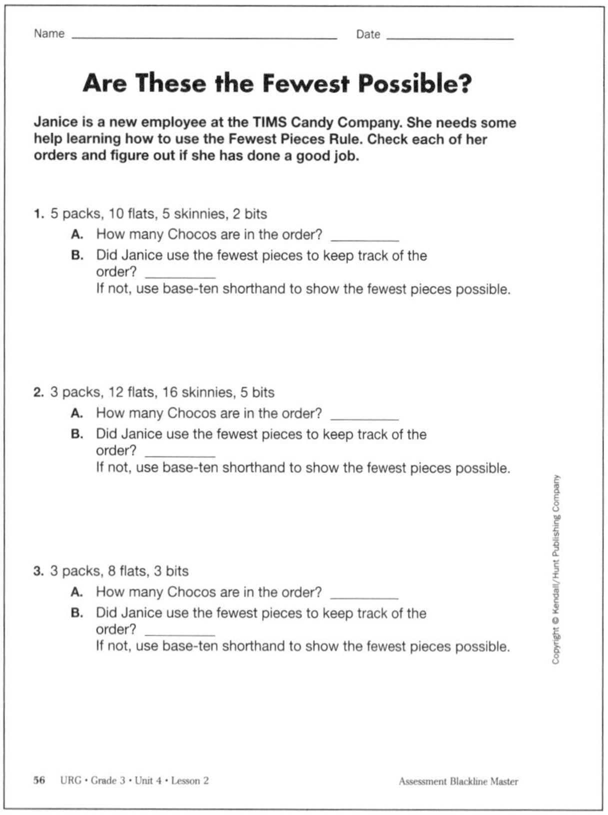

Name ______________ Date ______________

Are These the Fewest Possible?

Janice is a new employee at the TIMS Candy Company. She needs some help learning how to use the Fewest Pieces Rule. Check each of her orders and figure out if she has done a good job.

1. 5 packs, 10 flats, 5 skinnies, 2 bits
   - **A.** How many Chocos are in the order? ______
   - **B.** Did Janice use the fewest pieces to keep track of the order? ______
     If not, use base-ten shorthand to show the fewest pieces possible.

2. 3 packs, 12 flats, 16 skinnies, 5 bits
   - **A.** How many Chocos are in the order? ______
   - **B.** Did Janice use the fewest pieces to keep track of the order? ______
     If not, use base-ten shorthand to show the fewest pieces possible.

3. 3 packs, 8 flats, 3 bits
   - **A.** How many Chocos are in the order? ______
   - **B.** Did Janice use the fewest pieces to keep track of the order? ______
     If not, use base-ten shorthand to show the fewest pieces possible.

Copyright © Kendall/Hunt Publishing Company

56 URG • Grade 3 • Unit 4 • Lesson 2 Assessment Blackline Master

***Unit Resource Guide* - page 56**

Unit Resource Guide (p. 56)

Are These the Fewest Possible?

1. **A.** 6052 Chocos

   B. No

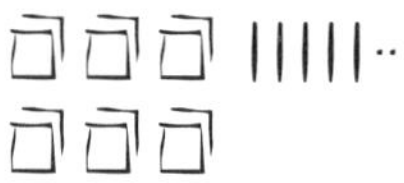

2. **A.** 4365

   B. No

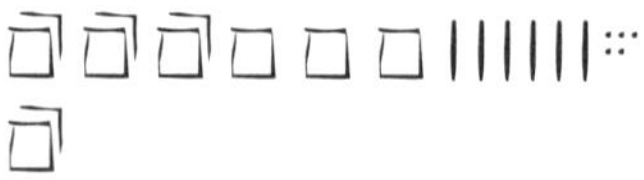

3. **A.** 3803

   B. Yes

Unit Resource Guide (p. 57)

Are They the Same?

1. No,

    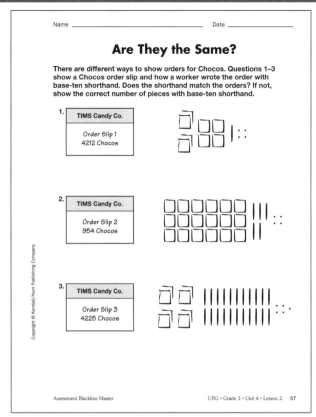

2. No,

3. No,

Unit Resource Guide - page 57

Lesson 3

Base-Ten Addition

Lesson Overview

Estimated Class Sessions

2

Students explore a standard addition algorithm while developing an understanding of place value. This activity concentrates on understanding two-digit plus two-digit addition.

Key Content

- Understanding place value.
- Solving addition problems and explaining mathematical reasoning.
- Representing addition problems using base-ten pieces.
- Adding multidigit numbers using manipulatives and drawings.
- Translating between representations of addition (base-ten pieces and symbols).

Key Vocabulary

- regrouping

Math Facts

DPP Bits K and M provide practice with the subtraction facts in Group 6.

Homework

1. Assign Part 4 of the Home Practice.
2. Students practice the subtraction facts in Group 6 using their flash cards.

Assessment

1. Students solve a problem and are assessed with the Student Rubric: *Knowing*.
2. Use Home Practice Part 3 as a quiz.

Curriculum Sequence

Before This Unit

Students represented addition and subtraction of two-digit numbers using base-ten pieces in Grade 2 Units 9 and 11.

After This Unit

In Grade 3 Unit 6 students will develop procedures for addition with three- and four-digit numbers. Students will review addition and subtraction of multidigit numbers in the Daily Practice and Problems, Home Practice, and in Unit 14 in the context of a reading survey.

Materials List

Supplies and Copies

Student	Teacher
Supplies for Each Student • 1 envelope for storing flash cards **Supplies for Each Student Pair or Group of Three** • 1 set of base-ten pieces	**Supplies**
Copies • 1 copy of *Base-Ten Board Part 1* and *Part 2* per student (*Unit Resource Guide* Pages 32–33) • 1 copy of *Base-Ten Recording Sheet* per student or more as needed (*Unit Resource Guide* Page 58)	**Copies/Transparencies** • 1 transparency of *Base-Ten Board Part 1* and *Part 2* (*Unit Resource Guide* Pages 32–33) • 1 transparency of *Base-Ten Recording Sheet* (*Unit Resource Guide* Page 58)

All blackline masters including assessment, transparency, and DPP masters are also on the Teacher Resource CD.

Student Books
Base-Ten Addition (*Student Guide* Pages 52–53)
Student Rubric: *Knowing* (*Student Guide* Appendix A and Inside Back Cover)
Subtraction Flash Cards: Group 6 (*Discovery Assignment Book* Pages 65–66)
Shortcut Addition (*Discovery Assignment Book* Pages 75–76)

Daily Practice and Problems and Home Practice
DPP items K–N (*Unit Resource Guide* Pages 18–20)
Home Practice Parts 3–4 (*Discovery Assignment Book* Page 61)

Note: Classrooms whose pacing differs significantly from the suggested pacing of the units should use the Math Facts Calendar in Section 4 of the *Facts Resource Guide* to ensure students receive the complete math facts program.

Daily Practice and Problems

Suggestions for using the DPPs are on page 75.

K. Bit: Subtraction: Thinking Addition
(URG p. 18)

Do these problems in your head. Write only the answers.

1. $6 - 4 =$
2. $6 - 2 =$
3. $13 - 5 =$
4. $8 - 5 =$
5. $8 - 3 =$
6. $13 - 8 =$
7. $12 - 8 =$
8. $12 - 4 =$
9. $12 - 3 =$

Update your *Subtraction Facts I Know* chart.

L. Challenge: $1000 to Share
(URG p. 19)

Suppose you had nine $100 bills and two $50 bills.

1. How could you divide the money into two shares? Write a number sentence for each way. (The shares don't have to be equal.)
2. How could you divide the money into three shares? Write a number sentence for each way.

M. Bit: Subtraction Flash Cards: Group 6 (URG p. 19)

1. With a partner, sort the flash cards into three stacks: Facts I Know Quickly, Facts I Know Using a Strategy, and Facts I Need to Learn.
2. Update your *Subtraction Facts I Know* chart. Circle the facts you answered quickly. Underline those you knew by using a strategy. Do nothing to those you still need to learn.

N. Challenge: Hot Dogs for Lunch
(URG p. 20)

Fifteen Cub Scouts are planning an overnight camping trip. Two fathers will also go. They will have hot dogs for lunch.

1. If each scout eats two hot dogs and each father eats three hot dogs, how many hot dogs will they need?
2. Buns come in packages of 8 that cost $1 and hot dogs come in packages of 8 that cost $2. How much will all the buns and hot dogs cost?

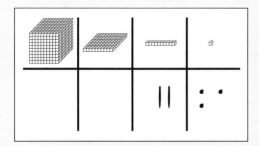

Figure 11: *Recording 2 skinnies and 3 bits using base-ten shorthand*

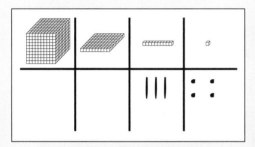

Figure 12: *Recording 34 Chocos using base-ten shorthand*

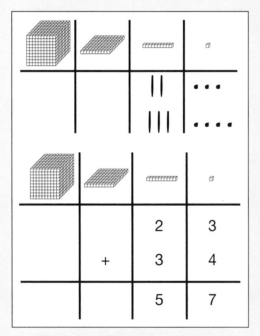

Figure 13: *Adding 23 and 34 on the Base-Ten Board*

If your students worked with base-ten pieces extensively in second grade, you may move quickly through the addition practice problems. It is, however, important to thoroughly cover the meaning of the columns and trading.

Encourage students to pretend they are helping Andy and Alda at the TIMS Candy Company. The company likes to keep track of all the Chocos made. One day, Andy made 23 Chocos. He recorded this as 2 skinnies and 3 bits as shown in Figure 11.

Alda made 34 Chocos. She recorded her work as 3 skinnies and 4 bits. See Figure 12.

Encourage students to find out how many Chocos they made altogether. Show both amounts on the board as shown in Figure 13. Since Andy has 3 bits and Alda has 4, there are 7 bits altogether. Andy has 2 skinnies, Alda has 3, and they have 5 skinnies altogether. Thus, Andy and Alda have 5 skinnies and 7 bits, or 57 Chocos altogether.

Challenge students to find out how many Chocos there would be if Andy showed his work as 23 bits and Alda showed hers as 34 bits. Students should realize that there would be 57 bits—the same amount of chocolate, just arranged or packaged differently.

Encourage students to complete other addition problems that do not involve **regrouping.** Each time, students should use base-ten pieces to model addends and shorthand to record their work. Instruct students to use their *Base-Ten Board* and *Base-Ten Recording Sheet.* Sample problems include those in Figure 14.

$$
\begin{array}{r} 1\ 3 \\ +\ 4\ 6 \\ \hline \end{array}
\qquad
\begin{array}{r} 5\ 2 \\ +\ \ \ 6 \\ \hline \end{array}
\qquad
\begin{array}{r} 6\ 9 \\ +\ 2\ 0 \\ \hline \end{array}
\qquad
\begin{array}{r} 2\ 5 \\ +\ 5\ 3 \\ \hline \end{array}
$$

Figure 14: *Problems without regrouping*

Stress that there may be other, simpler ways of finding solutions. For example, 69 + 20 can be solved by skip counting by tens. As students become comfortable modeling problems with base-ten pieces, explore other methods for finding solutions. It is good practice for students to do a problem several ways to verify that their solutions are correct.

Present problems with regrouping such as:

- *Andy made 36 Chocos and Alda made 29. Find how many Chocos they made altogether.*

Show the two amounts on the overhead. For example, Andy may make 3 skinnies and 6 bits while Alda makes 29 bits. Then write the corresponding amounts on the overhead on the *Base-Ten Recording Sheet.* Model the grouping and trading for students to follow. (29 bits plus 3 skinnies and 6 bits is 3 skinnies and 35 bits; 35 bits is 3 skinnies and 5 bits; 3 skinnies plus 3 skinnies and 5 bits is 6 skinnies and 5 bits, or 65 Chocos.) Record the solution. Ask students to confirm that the solution is correct. Check to see that the Fewest Pieces Rule is observed. Solve similar problems with regrouping using the Fewest Pieces Rule and record answers on the *Base-Ten Recording Sheet.* Sample problems include those in Figure 15.

$$
\begin{array}{r} 1\ 2 \\ +\ 1\ 8 \\ \hline \end{array}
\qquad
\begin{array}{r} 1\ 6 \\ +\ 1\ 5 \\ \hline \end{array}
\qquad
\begin{array}{r} 2\ 7 \\ +\ 3\ 4 \\ \hline \end{array}
\qquad
\begin{array}{r} 7\ 4 \\ +\ 1\ 7 \\ \hline \end{array}
$$

Figure 15: *Problems with regrouping*

Present problems that involve multiple regroupings such as

- *Andy made 58 Chocos and Alda made 65. How many did they make altogether?*

This problem will involve regrouping twice. When using blocks, it does not matter whether you start trading on the left or on the right. Two ways to present this problem are shown in Figure 16.

As a class, do several more problems that involve regrouping more than once. Then challenge students to solve some on their own. Each time students should use base-ten pieces on their *Base-Ten Boards* and *Base-Ten Recording Sheets.* Figure 17 shows sample problems.

$$
\begin{array}{r} 7\ 7 \\ +\ 4\ 4 \\ \hline \end{array}
\qquad
\begin{array}{r} 3\ 6 \\ +\ 9\ 7 \\ \hline \end{array}
\qquad
\begin{array}{r} 4\ 9 \\ +\ 5\ 5 \\ \hline \end{array}
\qquad
\begin{array}{r} 6\ 7 \\ +\ 5\ 3 \\ \hline \end{array}
$$

Figure 17: *Problems with multiple regroupings*

- *Solve 49 + 55 another way.* (Possible strategy: 49 + 1 + 54 = 50 + 54 = 104.)
- *Solve 67 + 53 another way.* (Possible strategy: 60 + 50 + 10 = 60 + 60 = 120.)

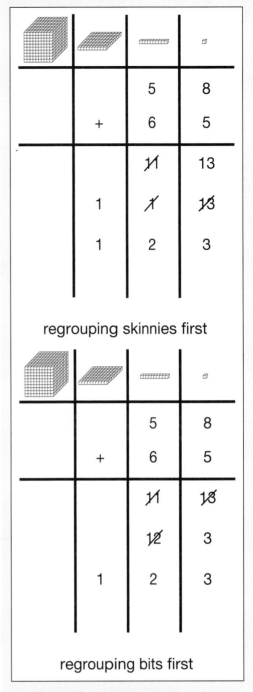

Figure 16: *Regrouping and trading using the Fewest Pieces Rule*

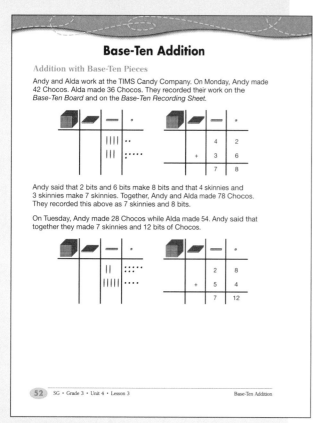

Student Guide - page 52

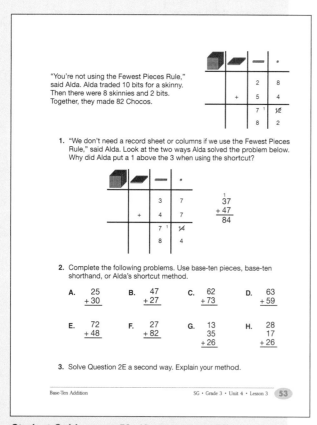

Student Guide - page 53 *(Answers on p. 78)*

If your students are ready, begin to move away from the column guides on the *Base-Ten Recording Sheet*. This prepares them for work with an algorithm. Ask students whether they think the column markings can always be eliminated. If they agree, offer a situation in which a misunderstanding could arise. For example, see Figure 18:

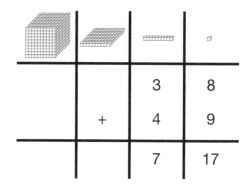

Figure 18: *Sample problem with necessary column markings*

Ask:

- *Can we just drop the columns and write 717?*
- *Could this mean 7 skinnies and 17 bits?*
- *Could it mean 7 packs, 1 flat, and 7 bits instead?*
- *How can we write it without the columns so that we know for sure what it represents?* (Use the Fewest Pieces Rule; trade 10 bits for one skinny, making 87.)

Explain that there are shortcut methods for adding—ways to compute sums with paper and pencil that do not involve drawing in columns. Your students may recognize a standard addition algorithm, or some other algorithm. Ask them if they have observed a parent or older sibling adding numbers.

You can introduce a standard addition algorithm as a method where the Fewest Pieces Rule is always observed. In the preceding problem, 38 was added to 49. If the bits are added first, we get 17 bits. However, this does not follow the Fewest Pieces Rule. So, arrange 17 bits as 1 skinny and 7 bits. Record 7 bits in the bits column. To keep track of a new skinny, put a small 1 in the skinnies column. Add up the skinnies to get 8. The answer is 87. See Figure 19.

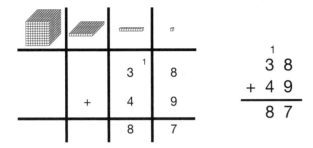

Figure 19: *Addition algorithm on the Base-Ten Board*

Try other problems such as those in Figure 20.

$$
\begin{array}{r} 2\ 5 \\ +\ 3\ 7 \\ \hline \end{array}
\qquad
\begin{array}{r} 4\ 5 \\ +\ 4\ 9 \\ \hline \end{array}
\qquad
\begin{array}{r} 5\ 3 \\ +\ 6\ 8 \\ \hline \end{array}
\qquad
\begin{array}{r} 7\ 2 \\ +\ 3\ 9 \\ \hline \end{array}
$$

Figure 20: *Sample problems with regrouping*

Encourage students to practice addition without column markings on the *Base-Ten Addition* Activity Pages in the *Student Guide* and the *Shortcut Addition* Activity Pages in the *Discovery Assignment Book*.

Math Facts

DPP Bits K and M provide practice with the subtraction facts in Group 6.

Homework and Practice

* Home Practice Part 4 is a set of problems involving time and money.
* For DPP Challenge L, students partition $1000. Challenge N is a multistep word problem.
* Remind students to take home their *Subtraction Flash Cards: Group 6* to practice with a family member.

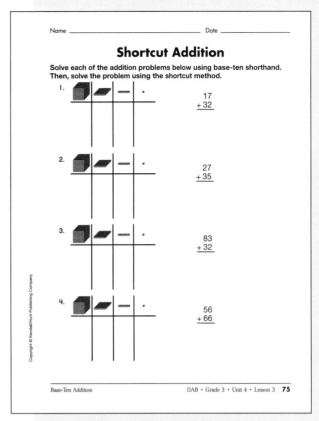

Discovery Assignment Book - page 75 *(Answers on p. 79)*

Discovery Assignment Book - page 76 *(Answers on p. 79)*

Name _____ Date _____

PART 3

1. Use base-ten shorthand to represent the following numbers:
   A. 76   B. 29

2. Riley counted 76 red cars while driving to the shopping mall with his dad. He counted 29 red cars on the way back home. How many red cars did he count? Show how you solved the problem.

3. Solve the problem a second way. Show your second method.

PART 4

1. Erin works part-time at the TIMS Candy Company. She punches in at 8 A.M. and punches out at 11:30 A.M. How many hours does she work?
   _____

2. A. Jayne has 7 dimes and 25 pennies. How much money does she have? _____
   B. If she traded the pennies for as many dimes as possible, how many dimes would she have in all?
   _____
   C. How many pennies would be left over? _____

3. Nathan has 3 dollars, 2 dimes, and 7 pennies. If he trades his money for all pennies, how many pennies will he have?
   _____

PLACE VALUE CONCEPTS   DAB • Grade 3 • Unit 4 **61**

Discovery Assignment Book - **page 61** *(Answers on p. 78)*

- Use the Student Rubric: *Knowing* to assess your students with the following problem:

  Kris breaks open his piggy bank and finds that he has 53 pennies, 28 dimes, 14 dollars, and 2 ten-dollar bills. How much money does Kris have in all? Point out to students the parallels between working with base-ten pieces and working with money. Have base-ten pieces available.

- Do students show that they have to regroup to find the solution using the Fewest Pieces Rule?

- Can students use a picture to describe the problem or model the problem using base-ten pieces?

- Do students use regrouping or base-ten pieces to do the problem?

- Do students use the addition facts to add correctly?

- Use Home Practice Part 3 as a quiz on adding with base-ten pieces.

Answers for Parts 3 and 4 of the Home Practice are in the Answer Key at the end of this lesson and at the end of this unit.

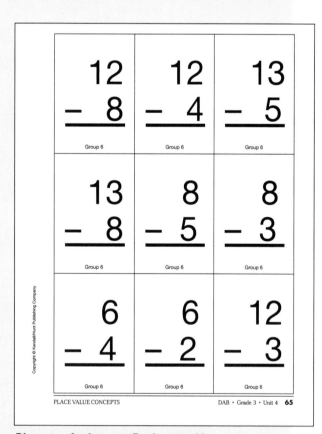

Discovery Assignment Book - **page 65**

At a Glance

Math Facts and Daily Practice and Problems

DPP Bits K and M provide practice with the subtraction facts in Group 6. Challenges L and N are multistep problems that use computations with money.

Teaching the Activity

1. Pass out base-ten pieces and copies of the *Base-Ten Board* and *Base-Ten Recording Sheet.*
2. Students solve problems without regrouping.
3. Students solve problems that involve regrouping one or more times.
4. Students discuss whether column markings are necessary to solve addition problems.
5. Students determine that column markings are not necessary if the Fewest Pieces Rule is observed.
6. Introduce a standard addition algorithm as a shortcut for adding on the *Base-Ten Recording Sheet.*
7. Students practice the addition algorithm on the *Base-Ten Addition* Activity Pages in the *Student Guide* and the *Shortcut Addition* Activity Pages in the *Discovery Assignment Book.*

Homework

1. Assign Part 4 of the Home Practice.
2. Students practice the subtraction facts in Group 6 using their flash cards.

Assessment

1. Students solve a problem and are assessed with the Student Rubric: *Knowing.*
2. Use Home Practice Part 3 as a quiz.

Answer Key is on pages 78–79.

Notes:

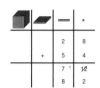

"You're not using the Fewest Pieces Rule," said Alda. Alda traded 10 bits for a skinny. Then there were 8 skinnies and 2 bits. Together, they made 82 Chocos.

	2	8
+	5	4
7 ^{1}	1̶2̶
8	2

1. "We don't need a record sheet or columns if we use the Fewest Pieces Rule," said Alda. Look at the two ways Alda solved the problem below. Why did Alda put a 1 above the 3 when using the shortcut?

	3	7
+	4	7
7 ^{1}	1̶4̶
8	4

$$\begin{array}{r} \overset{1}{3}7 \\ + 47 \\ \hline 84 \end{array}$$

2. Complete the following problems. Use base-ten pieces, base-ten shorthand, or Alda's shortcut method.

A. $\begin{array}{r} 25 \\ +30 \end{array}$ B. $\begin{array}{r} 47 \\ +27 \end{array}$ C. $\begin{array}{r} 62 \\ +73 \end{array}$ D. $\begin{array}{r} 63 \\ +59 \end{array}$

E. $\begin{array}{r} 72 \\ +48 \end{array}$ F. $\begin{array}{r} 27 \\ +82 \end{array}$ G. $\begin{array}{r} 13 \\ 35 \\ +26 \end{array}$ H. $\begin{array}{r} 28 \\ 17 \\ +26 \end{array}$

3. Solve Question 2E a second way. Explain your method.

Base-Ten Addition   SG • Grade 3 • Unit 4 • Lesson 3   **53**

Student Guide - page 53

Name _____ **Date** _____

PART 3
1. Use base-ten shorthand to represent the following numbers:
   A. 76   B. 29

2. Riley counted 76 red cars while driving to the shopping mall with his dad. He counted 29 red cars on the way back home. How many red cars did he count? Show how you solved the problem.

3. Solve the problem a second way. Show your second method.

PART 4
1. Erin works part-time at the TIMS Candy Company. She punches in at 8 A.M. and punches out at 11:30 A.M. How many hours does she work?
   _____

2. A. Jayne has 7 dimes and 25 pennies. How much money does she have? _____
   B. If she traded the pennies for as many dimes as possible, how many dimes would she have in all?
   _____
   C. How many pennies would be left over? _____

3. Nathan has 3 dollars, 2 dimes, and 7 pennies. If he trades his money for all pennies, how many pennies will he have?
   _____

PLACE VALUE CONCEPTS   DAB • Grade 3 • Unit 4   **61**

Discovery Assignment Book - page 61

Student Guide (p. 53)

1. Alda put a one above the three to show that she traded ten bits for one skinny.

2. **A.** 55   **B.** 74   **C.** 135
   D. 122   **E.** 120   **F.** 109
   G. 74   **H.** 71

3. Possible strategy: $70 + 40 + 10 = 120$.

Discovery Assignment Book (p. 61)

Home Practice*

Part 3

1. A. |||||⁚⁚⁚⁚⁚
      ||

   B. ||⁚⁚⁚⁚⁚

2. Possible method: Use base-ten shorthand

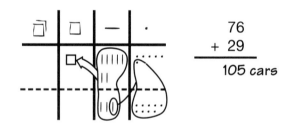

$$\begin{array}{r} 76 \\ + 29 \\ \hline 105 \text{ cars} \end{array}$$

3. Possible method:
   $76 + 29 = 75 + 30 = 105$ cars

Part 4

1. 3 and one half hours
2. **A.** 95¢   **B.** 9 dimes   **C.** 5 pennies
3. 327 pennies

*Answers for all the Home Practice in the *Discovery Assignment Book* are at the end of the unit.

Discovery Assignment Book (p. 75)

Shortcut Addition

1.
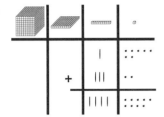

```
   1 7
 + 3 2
 ─────
   4 9
```

2.
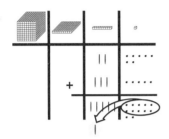

```
     1
   2 7
 + 3 5
 ─────
   6 2
```

3.
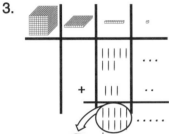

```
     1
   8 3
 + 3 2
 ─────
 1 1 5
```

4.
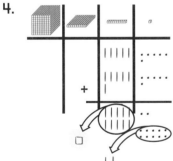

```
   1 1
   5 6
 + 6 6
 ─────
 1 2 2
```

Discovery Assignment Book (p. 76)

For *Questions 5–8,* methods will vary.

5. 80   **6.** 95   **7.** 92   **8.** 122

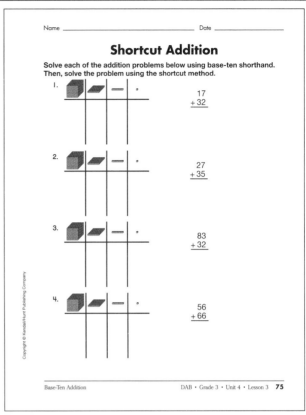

Discovery Assignment Book - page 75

Name _____ Date _____

Solve the problems in two ways. You may use base-ten shorthand,
Alda's shortcut method, or your own method.

5.   38
    + 42

6.   77
    + 18

7.   12
      35
    + 45

8.   40
    + 82

76   DAB • Grade 3 • Unit 4 • Lesson 3   Base-Ten Addition

Discovery Assignment Book - page 76

*Answers and/or discussion are included in the Lesson Guide.

Lesson 4

Bubble Sort

Estimated Class Sessions

I

Lesson Overview

Students arrange numbers in decreasing or increasing order.

Key Content
- Comparing and ordering numbers.
- Understanding place value.

Key Vocabulary
- bubble sort
- decreasing order
- increasing order

Assessment

Use the *Observational Assessment Record* to note students' abilities to compare and order large numbers.

Materials List

Supplies and Copies

Student	Teacher
Supplies for Each Student • 1 sheet of paper or index card	**Supplies**
Copies	**Copies/Transparencies**

All blackline masters including assessment, transparency, and DPP masters are also on the Teacher Resource CD.

Daily Practice and Problems and Home Practice

DPP items O–P (*Unit Resource Guide* Page 20)

Note: Classrooms whose pacing differs significantly from the suggested pacing of the units should use the Math Facts Calendar in Section 4 of the *Facts Resource Guide* to ensure students receive the complete math facts program.

Assessment Tools

Observational Assessment Record (*Unit Resource Guide* Pages 11–12)

Daily Practice and Problems

Suggestions for using the DPPs are on page 82.

O. Bit: Boxes (URG p. 20)

How are these boxes alike?

1		2	4		5	10		11
	10			22			46	
4		3	7		6	13		12

Make up two more boxes like these.

P. Task: Addition Practice (URG p. 20)

Solve each problem in two ways. Use base-ten pieces, base-ten shorthand, or a shortcut method.

1. $\begin{array}{r} 65 \\ +35 \\ \hline \end{array}$
2. $\begin{array}{r} 37 \\ +58 \\ \hline \end{array}$
3. $\begin{array}{r} 49 \\ +22 \\ \hline \end{array}$

Teaching the Activity

Ask students to write a number (up to four digits) on a piece of paper or index card. For greater variety, ask one-fourth of your class to write a one-digit number, one-fourth to write a two-digit number, one-fourth to write a three-digit number, and one-fourth to write a four-digit number. Tell students to line up with their numbers.

Explain that they will **bubble sort** with the head of the line as the largest number and the tail of the line as the smallest number. (The term "bubble sort" refers to the way that the larger numbers "bubble up" to the head of the line.) Have the first person and second person compare numbers. If the first person's number is larger, nothing is done. If the second person's number is larger than the first person's, then they are out of order and must switch places. Now the second person and third person compare numbers, and order themselves appropriately, then the third person compares with the fourth person, and so on.

Once the end of the line is reached, ask the class:

*   *Are you all in order?*
*   *Count off to check.*

Since it is likely that the numbers will not be in order, start at the head of the line and repeat the two-way comparisons a second time, switching whenever necessary. Have students check to see whether they are in order by asking them to count off again. Speed up the ordering process the third time. Instead of going down the line and making one comparison at a time, have pairs of adjacent students compare their numbers at the same time. Remind students that they can only switch with the person immediately to the right or left. Periodically ask students to stop and check the order by counting off. Repeat the procedure until the numbers are in order from largest to smallest. Then ask students to read their numbers aloud for a final check.

Homework and Practice

*   DPP items O and P provide practice with addition.
*   Remind students to continue practicing the subtraction facts for Groups 5 and 6 using their flash cards.

Assessment

Use the *Observational Assessment Record* to note students' abilities to order large numbers.

Math Facts and Daily Practice and Problems

DPP items O and P provide computation practice.

Teaching the Activity

1. Students write a number with four digits or less on a piece of paper or index card.
2. Students line up and compare their numbers with the person next to them. Pairs switch as necessary so that larger numbers move to the head of the line.
3. Students continue to bubble sort until no more switches are necessary.
4. Students read their numbers aloud to check the order.

Assessment

Use the *Observational Assessment Record* to note students' abilities to compare and order large numbers.

Notes:

Lesson 5

It's Time

Students practice telling time to the nearest five minutes. They make a clock and use it to review the position of the hour and minute hands for various times of day. Students use the context of the TIMS Candy Company to practice writing and telling time on analog and digital clocks. They will continue to practice this skill in the Daily Practice and Problems for this and succeeding units.

Key Content

• Telling time to the nearest five minutes.

Key Vocabulary

• A.M.
• analog clock
• digital clock
• P.M.

Math Facts

DPP items S and T provide practice with math facts.

Homework

Assign some or all of the Lesson 6 problems.

Assessment

Students complete the *Time* Assessment Page.

Curriculum Sequence

Before This Unit

Students began telling time to the nearest half hour in Grade 2 Unit 6 Lesson 1. They practiced telling time throughout the year in the Daily Practice and Problems.

After This Unit

In Grade 3 Unit 14 students will tell time to the nearest minute. They will practice telling time and solving problems involving time in the Daily Practice and Problems and Home Practice.

Materials List

Supplies and Copies

Student	Teacher
Supplies for Each Student • scissors • brass fastener	**Supplies** • analog demonstration clock
Copies • 1 copy of *Time* per student (*Unit Resource Guide* Page 93)	**Copies/Transparencies**

All blackline masters including assessment, transparency, and DPP masters are also on the Teacher Resource CD.

Student Books

It's Time (*Student Guide* Pages 54–55)
Clock (*Discovery Assignment Book* Page 77)

Daily Practice and Problems and Home Practice

DPP items Q–T (*Unit Resource Guide* Pages 21–22)

Note: Classrooms whose pacing differs significantly from the suggested pacing of the units should use the Math Facts Calendar in Section 4 of the *Facts Resource Guide* to ensure students receive the complete math facts program.

Daily Practice and Problems

Suggestions for using the DPPs are on page 91.

Q. Bit: Coins (URG p. 21)

Marcus buys an apple for 45¢. He used 5 coins to pay for it. He didn't get any change back. What coins did he use?

Can you find more than one solution?

R. Challenge: Beans for Dinner
(URG p. 21)

Fifteen Cub Scouts are planning an overnight camping trip. Two fathers will also go. They will have beans for dinner.

1. If three scouts share a can of beans and the two fathers share a can, how many cans of beans will they need?
2. If each can of beans costs 50¢, how much will the beans cost?

S. Bit: More Subtraction (URG p. 21)

Do these problems in your head. Write only the answers.

1. 60 − 40 =
2. 60 − 20 =
3. 500 − 200 =
4. 80 − 60 =
5. 80 − 50 =
6. 80 − 30 =
7. 12 − 3 =
8. 120 − 30 =
9. 110 − 20 =

T. Task: Story Solving (URG p. 22)

$3 \times 6 = ?$ Write a story and draw a picture about 3×6. Write a number sentence on your picture.

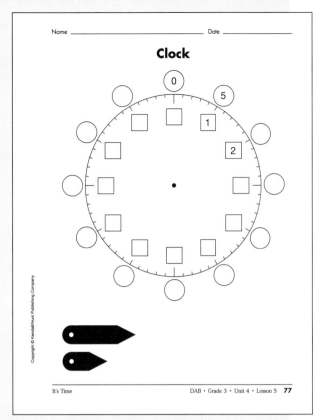

Inside the activity page image:

Name _____ Date _____

Clock

0

5

1

2

Copyright © Kendall/Hunt Publishing Company

It's Time

DAB • Grade 3 • Unit 4 • Lesson 5   **77**

Teaching the Activity

Part 1 The Hands on a Clock

Review the position of the hour hand on an **analog clock** for various times of the day. Instruct students to fill in the hours on the *Clock* Activity Page in the *Discovery Assignment Book* by writing the numbers three through twelve in the squares. Students then cut out the hour hand and fasten it to the clock with a brass fastener. Use the following questions to guide students as they work with the clock. Each time you ask a question that has a time in it, students should show the position of the hour hand for the time mentioned.

- *How many hours are in a day?* (24)
- *How many hours are shown on the clock?* (12)
- *If there are 24 hours in a day and only 12 hours on the clock, what do we do about the other 12 hours?* (We put A.M. after the hours before noon and P.M. after the hours following noon. For example, we say "8:00 A.M." or "eight o'clock in the morning.")
- *Where will the hour hand point if it is 12:00 midnight? Show me on your clock.*
- *Where will the hour hand point one hour later?*
- *Where will the hour hand point at 8:00 A.M.?*
- *Where will the hour hand point at 8:30?*
- *Where will the hour hand point just before 9:00?*
- *Where will the hour hand point at 12:00 noon?*
- *How many times does the hour hand go around the clock in one day?*

Continue to ask students to show positions of the hour hand for other times until they are ready to begin discussing the minute hand. Use the following questions:

- *How many minutes are in one hour?* (60)
- *How many lines are there around the clock?* (60)
- *Is there an easy way to count the lines?* (The longer lines show the fives, so you can skip count by fives.)

Ask students to fill in the circles on the *Clock* Activity Page by skip counting by fives around the clock face. Then they can cut out the minute hand, undo the brass fastener, and refasten it with both the minute and hour hands attached. Encourage students to use their clocks as you pose the following questions:

- *How is your clock different from the classroom clock?* (The classroom clock doesn't have 5, 10, 15, 20, and so on written for the minute numbers.)

- *How can you use your clock to multiply by five?* (When the numbers written in the squares are multiplied by five, the answers are the numbers written in the circles.)

- *Show 8:00 on your clock. Count by "5 minutes" from 8:00 to 8:30. Show each time on your clock.* (Eight o five, eight ten, eight fifteen, etc.) (As students work with the clock, they should concentrate on the minute hand. However, you may wish to remind them that the hour hand will be halfway between the numbers 8 and 9 at 8:30.)

- *Continue counting by 5 minutes from 8:30 to 9:00.*

- *Show 3:30 on your clock. What is another way to tell someone it is 3:30?* (Half past three.)

- *Show 1:15 on your clock. What is another way to say 1:15?* (Fifteen minutes past one.)

- *Can someone tell me yet another way?* (Quarter after one.)

- *Why do some people say "quarter after"?* (If you divide the clock into fourths, or quarters, you can see that the minute hand will move through one-fourth of the clock in 15 minutes.)

- *Show 1:45 on your clock. What is another way to say 1:45?* (45 minutes after 1:00, three quarters past 1:00)

- *What hour are we getting close to?* (2:00)

- *How many minutes until we get to 2:00?* (fifteen minutes)

- *Can we say that another way to say 1:45 is fifteen minutes before 2:00?* (yes)

- *What time does school start? Show this time on your clocks.* (Ask students to practice using A.M. and P.M. if appropriate.)

- *What time does school end? Show this time on your clocks.*

- *What time do we go to gym (art, music, lunch, etc.)?*

- *How long does gym (art, music, lunch, etc.) last?*

- *What time is gym (art, music, lunch, etc.) over?*

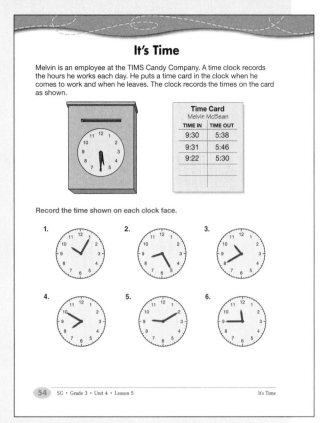

Student Guide - page 54 *(Answers on p. 94)*

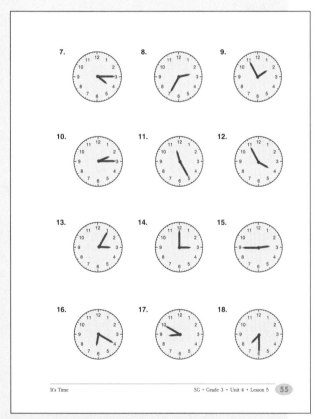

Student Guide - page 55 *(Answers on p. 94)*

Show several times in five-minute increments, such as 4:10, 5:25, 6:05, 7:40, 8:50. Have students repeat the times after you and say them different ways, for example, "four ten" and "ten minutes after four."

• *Show 3:55 on your clock. Show 11:20 on your clock. How can you tell the difference between the two times?* (The hands are reversed. You can tell the difference by the size of the hands and the slight difference in position.)

Part 2 **The Clocks at the TIMS Candy Company**

Discuss the similarities and differences between analog and **digital clocks.** Describe the features of each type of clock. Ask students where they have seen digital and analog clocks. The *It's Time* Activity Pages have an illustration of the time clock the employees of the TIMS Candy Company use to record the hours they work each day. Time clocks have both analog and digital features. The clock face on the front of a time clock is often analog, but when an employee puts a time card into the clock to "punch in," the time is usually displayed in digital numbers. Discuss the use of a time clock with your students.

Model 3:25 on the analog demonstration clock. Ask students to write the time that will be reported on the workers' time cards. You may need to review writing time using a colon. Model other times for students to identify and write. Students complete the *It's Time* Activity Pages in the *Student Guide.*

Math Facts

DPP items S and T both provide practice with math facts. Bit S provides practice subtracting with ending zeros. Task T involves writing a story and drawing a picture to illustrate a multiplication fact.

Homework and Practice

- DPP Bit Q provides practice with money. Challenge R is a multistep word problem that provides computation practice.

- Assign some or all of the problems in Lesson 6 *Time for Problems* for homework.

Assessment

Use the *Time* Assessment Page to assess telling time and solving problems involving elapsed time. You can give this assessment to students now, or after students complete more of the time DPP items in succeeding units.

Literature Connection

- Hutchins, Pat. *Clocks and More Clocks*. Aladdin Library, Hong Kong, 1994.

This is a story about a man who finds a clock in his attic and becomes confused when he tries to check the time on it by using clocks in other parts of his house. He reads a clock on another floor and then runs to the attic, only to find that the times are not the same. The illustrations include many clock faces so students can practice telling time as they read the story.

At a Glance

Math Facts and Daily Practice and Problems

DPP items S and T provide practice with math facts. Items Q and R provide computation practice with money.

Part 1. The Hands on a Clock

1. Students label the hours, cut out the hour hand, and attach it with a brass fastener on their *Clock* Activity Page in the *Discovery Assignment Book.*
2. Students model and tell time on their clocks while answering questions about time.
3. Students fill in the minutes and attach the minute hand on their clocks.
4. Students show and read times to the nearest five minutes.

Part 2. The Clocks at the TIMS Candy Company

1. Students discuss attributes of digital and analog clocks.
2. Students complete the problems on the *It's Time* Activity Pages.

Homework

Assign some or all of the Lesson 6 problems.

Assessment

Students complete the *Time* Assessment Page.

Connection

Read and discuss *Clocks and More Clocks* by Pat Hutchins.

Answer Key is on pages 94–95.

Notes:

Name _____ Date _____

Time

Write the time shown on each clock.

1._____ **2.**_____ **3.**_____

Answer the following questions in hours and minutes. Then, explain how you found your answers.

4. Shanta came to baby-sit at 5:15 P.M. She left at 8:00 P.M. How long did she baby-sit?

5. Joe's little brother took a nap at 1:30 P.M. He woke up at 4:30 P.M. How long did he sleep?

6. Kris practices the tuba for 20 minutes every day. How much does he practice in a week? Give your answer in hours and minutes.

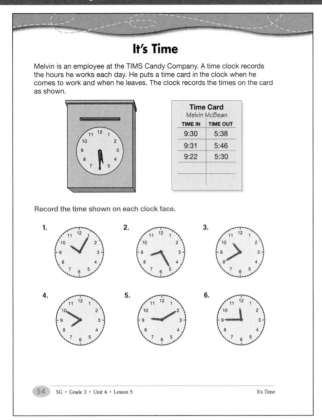

Student Guide - page 54

Student Guide (p. 54)

It's Time

1. 10:05
2. 8:25
3. 10:40
4. 7:50
5. 9:10
6. 11:45

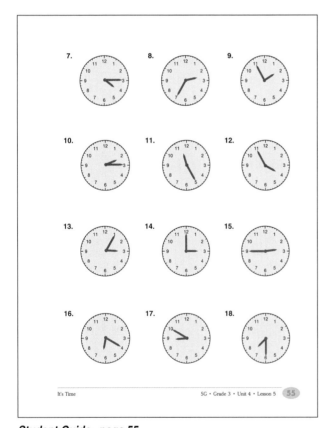

Student Guide - page 55

Student Guide (p. 55)

7. 4:15
8. 2:35
9. 1:55
10. 2:15
11. 11:25
12. 3:55
13. 3:05
14. 3:00
15. 2:45
16. 6:20
17. 8:50
18. 7:30

Unit Resource Guide (p. 93)

Time

1. 1:15

2. 8:25

3. 5:55 or five minutes before 6:00

4. 2 hours, 45 minutes

5. 3 hours

6. 2 hours, 20 minutes

(7 × 20 = 140 minutes; 2 hrs = 120 minutes, 20 minutes left over.)

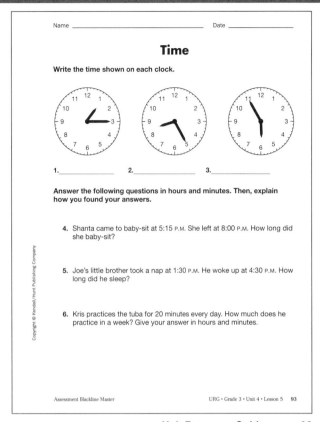

Name _____ Date _____

Time

Write the time shown on each clock.

1._____ 2._____ 3._____

Answer the following questions in hours and minutes. Then, explain how you found your answers.

4. Shanta came to baby-sit at 5:15 P.M. She left at 8:00 P.M. How long did she baby-sit?

5. Joe's little brother took a nap at 1:30 P.M. He woke up at 4:30 P.M. How long did he sleep?

6. Kris practices the tuba for 20 minutes every day. How much does he practice in a week? Give your answer in hours and minutes.

Assessment Blackline Master   URG • Grade 3 • Unit 4 • Lesson 5   93

Unit Resource Guide - page 93

Lesson 6

Time for Problems

Lesson Overview

This lesson is a series of word problems about telling time and elapsed time. To solve them, students use the analog clock they constructed in Lesson 5.

Key Content

- Solving problems involving elapsed time.
- Skip counting.
- Connecting mathematics to real-life situations.

Homework

Assign some or all of the *Time for Problems* as homework.

Assessment

1. Use DPP Bit U as an assessment.
2. Use the *Observational Assessment Record* to note students' abilities to tell time to the nearest five minutes.
3. Transfer appropriate documentation from the Unit 4 *Observational Assessment Record* to students' *Individual Assessment Record Sheets*.

Materials List

Supplies and Copies

Student	Teacher
Supplies for Each Student • analog clock from Lesson 5	**Supplies**
Copies	**Copies/Transparencies**

All blackline masters including assessment, transparency, and DPP masters are also on the Teacher Resource CD.

Student Books

Time for Problems (*Student Guide* Page 56)

Daily Practice and Problems and Home Practice

DPP items U–V (*Unit Resource Guide* Page 22)

Note: Classrooms whose pacing differs significantly from the suggested pacing of the units should use the Math Facts Calendar in Section 4 of the *Facts Resource Guide* to ensure students receive the complete math facts program.

Assessment Tools

Observational Assessment Record (*Unit Resource Guide* Pages 11–12)
Individual Assessment Record Sheet (*Teacher Implementation Guide,* Assessment section)

Daily Practice and Problems

Suggestions for using the DPPs are on page 98.

U. Bit: More Boxes (URG p. 22)

What is special about these boxes?

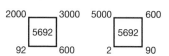

1. Make up another box for 5692.
2. Show 5692 using base-ten shorthand.

V. Challenge: Addition Squares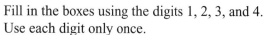
(URG p. 22)

Fill in the boxes using the digits 1, 2, 3, and 4.
Use each digit only once.

□ □ + □ □

1. What is the largest sum you can get?
2. What is the smallest sum you can get?
3. How many different sums can you find?

Student Guide - page 56 *(Answers on p. 100)*

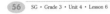

Teaching the Activity

A goal for students is to develop the ability to analyze word problems critically and to choose appropriate methods for solving them. The problems in this lesson involve telling time to the nearest five minutes and calculating elapsed time. To solve them, students should use the analog clocks they constructed in Lesson 5 and any other tools or methods they find helpful. Skip counting by fives is an efficient strategy. Students will be reminded to use this strategy by seeing the numbers they have written in the circles on their clocks.

As students encounter different kinds of word problems in their mathematical studies, they will learn many diverse and effective problem-solving tools to use when confronting unfamiliar problems. For further information about word problem sets, see the TIMS Tutor: *Word Problems* in the *Teacher Implementation Guide.*

Using the Problems. Students can work on the problems individually, in pairs, or in groups. One approach is to ask them to work individually at first and then to come together in pairs or small groups to compare solutions. Then, solutions can be shared with others in a class discussion. You can also assign the problems for homework. Because this activity does not require much teacher preparation, it is appropriate to leave for a substitute teacher.

Homework and Practice

- DPP Challenge V builds number sense and computation skills.
- Some or all of the *Time for Problems* can be assigned as homework.

Assessment

- Use DPP Bit U as a quick assessment of students' abilities to partition numbers and represent them using base-ten shorthand.
- Use the *Observational Assessment Record* to note students' abilities to tell time to the nearest five minutes.
- Transfer appropriate documentation from the Unit 4 *Observational Assessment Record* to students' *Individual Assessment Record Sheets.*

At a Glance

Math Facts and Daily Practice and Problems

DPP item U provides practice with partitioning numbers and writing base-ten shorthand and can be used as an assessment. Item V builds number sense and computational skills.

Teaching the Activity

1. Students use their analog clocks from Lesson 5 to solve the problems on the *Time for Problems* Activity Page in the *Student Guide.*
2. Students write their answers on a separate sheet of paper.

Homework

Assign some or all of the *Time for Problems* as homework.

Assessment

1. Use DPP Bit U as an assessment.
2. Use the *Observational Assessment Record* to note students' abilities to tell time to the nearest five minutes.
3. Transfer appropriate documentation from the Unit 4 *Observational Assessment Record* to students' *Individual Assessment Record Sheets.*

Answer Key is on page 100.

Notes:

Time for Problems

Use your student clock to complete the following problems. Remember to use skip counting by fives.

1. The hour hand is just before the two. The minute hand is pointing to the eight. What time is it?

2. What is another way to say the time 6:45?

3. Martha left school at 3:15 P.M. It takes her 15 minutes to walk home. What time should Martha arrive at home?

4. Shelby looked at her watch. The time was 3:25 P.M. Shelby has to be home at 4:00 P.M. How much time does Shelby still have to play outside?

5. School starts in Lincolnshire at 8:30 A.M. Draw a picture of a clock with hands showing 8:30 A.M.

6. Stacy looked at her watch. How could Stacy find out how many minutes are in one hour without counting each minute mark?

7. Marcus has band practice from 3:30 P.M. to 4:15 P.M. How many minutes does Marcus have band practice?

8. Math class starts at 1:20 P.M. It lasts 50 minutes. What time does math class end?

9. Frieda's soccer team usually practices 45 minutes. Today, Frieda's coach said, "Let's practice 15 minutes longer." How long did Frieda practice today?

10. Enrique looked at his watch. The hour hand is between the two and the three. The minute hand is pointing to the five. What time is on Enrique's watch?

56   SG • Grade 3 • Unit 4 • Lesson 6   Time for Problems

Student Guide - page 56

Student Guide (p. 56)

Time for Problems

1. 1:40

2. Answers will vary. Three-quarters past the hour, 15 minutes to seven

3. 3:30

4. thirty-five minutes

5.

6. Answers will vary. Stacy could skip count by fives.

7. 45 minutes

8. 2:10

9. 1 hour or 60 minutes

10. 2:25

Discovery Assignment Book (p. 60)

Part 1

I. **A.** 8

B. 48

C. 68

2. **A.** 11

B. 51

C. 131

3.

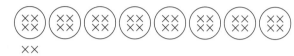

$\times\times$

$8 \times 4 + 2 = 34$

4. **A.** 100, 110, 120, 130, 140, 150, 160, 170, 180, 190, 200, 210, 220, 230, 240, 250, 260, 270, 280, 290, 300

B. 100, 200, 300, 400, 500, 600, 700, 800, 900, 1000

Part 2

I. **A.** 60

B. 70

C. 20

2. **A.** 90

B. 120

C. 80

3. Answers will vary.

A. $79 = 59 + 20$

B. $507 = 500 + 7$

$507 = 100 + 400 + 7$

C. $1551 = 1000 + 500 + 51$

$1551 = 1000 + 500 + 50 + 1$

Name _____ Date _____

Unit 4 Home Practice

PART 1

1. **A.** 12 − 4 = _____   2. **A.** 3 + 8 = _____
   B. 52 − 4 = _____   **B.** 43 + 8 = _____
   C. 72 − 4 = _____   **C.** 123 + 8 = _____

3. Alicia's class has 34 students in it. Draw a picture to show how many teams of four can be formed. Write a number sentence to describe this problem.

4. **A.** Skip count by tens from 100 to 300.
   _____

   B. Skip count by hundreds from 100 to 1000.
   _____

PART 2

1. **A.** 80 − 20 = _____   2. **A.** 110 − 20 = _____
   B. 30 + 40 = _____   **B.** 30 + 90 = _____
   C. 50 − 30 = _____   **C.** 130 − 50 = _____

3. Break the following numbers into two, three, or four parts.
   A. 79 = _____ + _____
   B. 507 = _____ + _____
      507 = _____ + _____ + _____
   C. 1551 = _____ + _____ + _____
      1551 = _____ + _____ + _____ + _____

60 DAB • Grade 3 • Unit 4   PLACE VALUE CONCEPTS

Discovery Assignment Book - page 60

Name _____ Date _____

PART 3

1. Use base-ten shorthand to represent the following numbers:
   A. 76   B. 29

2. Riley counted 76 red cars while driving to the shopping mall with his dad. He counted 29 red cars on the way back home. How many red cars did he count? Show how you solved the problem.

3. Solve the problem a second way. Show your second method.

PART 4

1. Erin works part-time at the TIMS Candy Company. She punches in at 8 A.M. and punches out at 11:30 A.M. How many hours does she work?
   _____

2. A. Jayne has 7 dimes and 25 pennies. How much money does she have? _____
   B. If she traded the pennies for as many dimes as possible, how many dimes would she have in all?
   _____
   C. How many pennies would be left over? _____

3. Nathan has 3 dollars, 2 dimes, and 7 pennies. If he trades his money for all pennies, how many pennies will he have?
   _____

PLACE VALUE CONCEPTS   DAB • Grade 3 • Unit 4   **61**

Discovery Assignment Book - page 61

Discovery Assignment Book (p. 61)

Part 3

1. A. |||||⁚⁚⁚⁚
      ||

   B. ||⁚⁚⁚⁚⁚

2. Possible method: Use base-ten shorthand

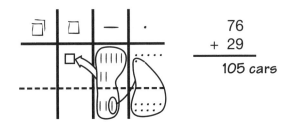

$$\begin{array}{r} 76 \\ + 29 \\ \hline 105 \ cars \end{array}$$

3. Possible method:
   $76 + 29 = 75 + 30 = 105$ cars

Part 4

1. 3 and one-half hours
2. A. 95¢
   B. 9 dimes
   C. 5 pennies
3. 327 pennies

Glossary

This glossary provides definitions of key vocabulary terms in the Grade 3 lessons. Locations of key vocabulary terms in the curriculum are included with each definition. Components Key: URG = *Unit Resource Guide,* SG = *Student Guide,* and DAB = *Discovery Assignment Book.*

A

Area (URG Unit 5; SG Unit 5)
The area of a shape is the amount of space it covers, measured in square units.

Array (URG Unit 7 & Unit 11)
An array is an arrangement of elements into a rectangular pattern of (horizontal) rows and (vertical) columns. (*See* column and row.)

Associative Property of Addition (URG Unit 2)
For any three numbers a, b, and c we have $a + (b + c) = (a + b) + c$. For example in finding the sum of 4, 8, and 2, one can compute $4 + 8$ first and then add 2: $(4 + 8) + 2 = 14$. Alternatively, we can compute $8 + 2$ and then add the result to 4: $4 + (8 + 2) = 4 + 10 = 14$.

Average (URG Unit 5)
A number that can be used to represent a typical value in a set of data. (*See also* mean and median.)

Axes (URG Unit 8; SG Unit 8)
Reference lines on a graph. In the Cartesian coordinate system, the axes are two perpendicular lines that meet at the origin. The singular of axes is axis.

B

Base (of a cube model) (URG Unit 18; SG Unit 18)
The part of a cube model that sits on the "ground."

Base-Ten Board (URG Unit 4)
A tool to help children organize base-ten pieces when they are representing numbers.

Base-Ten Pieces (URG Unit 4; SG Unit 4)
A set of manipulatives used to model our number system as shown in the figure at the right. Note that a skinny is made of 10 bits, a flat is made of 100 bits, and a pack is made of 1000 bits.

Base-Ten Shorthand (SG Unit 4)
A pictorial representation of the base-ten pieces as shown.

Nickname	Picture	Shorthand
bit		·
skinny		/
flat		
pack		

Best-Fit Line (URG Unit 9; SG Unit 9; DAB Unit 9)
The line that comes closest to the most number of points on a point graph.

Bit (URG Unit 4; SG Unit 4)
A cube that measures 1 cm on each edge. It is the smallest of the base-ten pieces that is often used to represent 1. (*See also* base-ten pieces.)

C

Capacity (URG Unit 16)
1. The volume of the inside of a container.
2. The largest volume a container can hold.

Cartesian Coordinate System (URG Unit 8)
A method of locating points on a flat surface by means of numbers. This method is named after its originator, René Descartes. (*See also* coordinates.)

Centimeter (cm)
A unit of measure in the metric system equal to one-hundredth of a meter. (1 inch = 2.54 cm)

Column (URG Unit 11)
In an array, the objects lined up vertically.

column 3

Common Fraction (URG Unit 15)
Any fraction that is written with a numerator and denominator that are whole numbers. For example, $\frac{3}{4}$ and $\frac{9}{4}$ are both common fractions. (*See also* decimal fraction.)

Commutative Property of Addition (URG Unit 2 & Unit 11)
This is also known as the Order Property of Addition. Changing the order of the addends does not change the sum. For example, $3 + 5 = 5 + 3 = 8$. Using variables, $n + m = m + n$.

Commutative Property of Multiplication (URG Unit 11)
Changing the order of the factors in a multiplication problem does not change the result, e.g., $7 \times 3 = 3 \times 7 = 21$. (*See also* turn-around facts.)

Congruent (URG Unit 12 & Unit 17; SG Unit 12)
Figures with the same shape and size.

Convenient Number (URG Unit 6)
A number used in computation that is close enough to give a good estimate, but is also easy to compute mentally, e.g., 25 and 30 are convenient numbers for 27.

Coordinates (URG Unit 8; SG Unit 8)
An ordered pair of numbers that locates points on a flat surface by giving distances from a pair of coordinate axes. For example, if a point has coordinates (4, 5) it is 4 units from the vertical axis and 5 units from the horizontal axis.

Counting Back (URG Unit 2)
A strategy for subtracting in which students start from a larger number and then count down until the number is reached. For example, to solve $8 - 3$, begin with 8 and count down three, 7, 6, 5.

Counting Down (*See* counting back.)

Counting Up (URG Unit 2)
A strategy for subtraction in which the student starts at the lower number and counts on to the higher number. For example, to solve $8 - 5$, the student starts at 5 and counts up three numbers (6, 7, 8). So $8 - 5 = 3$.

Cube (SG Unit 18)
A three-dimensional shape with six congruent square faces.

Cubic Centimeter (cc)
(URG Unit 16; SG Unit 16)
The volume of a cube that is one centimeter long on each edge.

cubic centimeter

Cup (URG Unit 16)
A unit of volume equal to 8 fluid ounces, one-half pint.

D

Decimal Fraction (URG Unit 15)
A fraction written as a decimal. For example, 0.75 and 0.4 are decimal fractions and $\frac{75}{100}$ and $\frac{4}{10}$ are called common fractions. (*See also* fraction.)

Denominator (URG Unit 13)
The number below the line in a fraction. The denominator indicates the number of equal parts in which the unit whole is divided. For example, the 5 is the denominator in the fraction $\frac{2}{5}$. In this case the unit whole is divided into five equal parts.

Density (URG Unit 16)
The ratio of an object's mass to its volume.

Difference (URG Unit 2)
The answer to a subtraction problem.

Dissection (URG Unit 12 & Unit 17)
Cutting or decomposing a geometric shape into smaller shapes that cover it exactly.

Distributive Property of Multiplication over Addition (URG Unit 19)
For any three numbers a, b, and c, $a \times (b + c) = a \times b + a \times c$. The distributive property is the foundation for most methods of multidigit multiplication. For example, $9 \times (17) = 9 \times (10 + 7) = 9 \times 10 + 9 \times 7 = 90 + 63 = 153$.

E

Equal-Arm Balance
See two-pan balance.

Equilateral Triangle (URG Unit 7)
A triangle with all sides of equal length and all angles of equal measure.

Equivalent Fractions (SG Unit 17)
Fractions that have the same value, e.g., $\frac{2}{4} = \frac{1}{2}$.

Estimate (URG Unit 5 & Unit 6)
1. (verb) To find *about* how many.
2. (noun) An approximate number.

Extrapolation (URG Unit 7)
Using patterns in data to make predictions or to estimate values that lie beyond the range of values in the set of data.

F

Fact Family (URG Unit 11; SG Unit 11)
Related math facts, e.g., $3 \times 4 = 12$, $4 \times 3 = 12$, $12 \div 3 = 4$, $12 \div 4 = 3$.

Factor (URG Unit 11; SG Unit 11)
1. In a multiplication problem, the numbers that are multiplied together. In the problem $3 \times 4 = 12$, 3 and 4 are the factors.
2. Whole numbers that can be multiplied together to get a number. That is, numbers that divide a number evenly, e.g., 1, 2, 3, 4, 6, and 12 are all the factors of 12.

Fewest Pieces Rule (URG Unit 4 & Unit 6; SG Unit 4)
Using the least number of base-ten pieces to represent a number. (*See also* base-ten pieces.)

Flat (URG Unit 4; SG Unit 4)
A block that measures 1 cm $\times$ 10 cm $\times$ 10 cm. It is one of the base-ten pieces that is often used to represent 100. (*See also* base-ten pieces.)

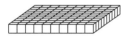

Flip (URG Unit 12)
A motion of the plane in which a figure is reflected over a line so that any point and its image are the same distance from the line.

Fraction (URG Unit 15)
A number that can be written as $\frac{a}{b}$ where a and b are whole numbers and b is not zero. For example, $\frac{1}{2}$, 0.5, and 2 are all fractions since 0.5 can be written as $\frac{5}{10}$ and 2 can be written as $\frac{2}{1}$.

Front-End Estimation (URG Unit 6)
Estimation by looking at the left-most digit.

G

Gallon (gal) (URG Unit 16)
A unit of volume equal to four quarts.

Gram
The basic unit used to measure mass.

H

Hexagon (SG Unit 12)
A six-sided polygon.

Horizontal Axis (SG Unit 1)
In a coordinate grid, the x-axis. The axis that extends from left to right.

I

Interpolation (URG Unit 7)
Making predictions or estimating values that lie between data points in a set of data.

J

K

Kilogram
1000 grams.

L

Likely Event (SG Unit 1)
An event that has a high probability of occurring.

Line of Symmetry (URG Unit 12)
A line is a line of symmetry for a plane figure if, when the figure is folded along this line, the two parts match exactly.

Line Symmetry (URG Unit 12; SG Unit 12)
A figure has line symmetry if it has at least one line of symmetry.

Liter (l) (URG Unit 16; SG Unit 16)
Metric unit used to measure volume. A liter is a little more than a quart.

M

Magic Square (URG Unit 2)
A square array of digits in which the sums of the rows, columns, and main diagonals are the same.

Making a Ten (URG Unit 2)
Strategies for addition and subtraction that make use of knowing the sums to ten. For example, knowing $6 + 4 = 10$ can be helpful in finding $10 - 6 = 4$ and $11 - 6 = 5$.

Mass (URG Unit 9 & Unit 16; SG Unit 9)
The amount of matter in an object.

Mean (URG Unit 5)
An average of a set of numbers that is found by adding the values of the data and dividing by the number of values.

Measurement Division (URG Unit 7)
Division as equal grouping. The total number of objects and the number of objects in each group are known. The number of groups is the unknown. For example, tulip bulbs come in packages of 8. If 216 bulbs are sold, how many packages are sold?

Measurement Error (URG Unit 9)
The unavoidable error that occurs due to the limitations inherent to any measurement instrument.

Median (URG Unit 5; DAB Unit 5)
For a set with an odd number of data arranged in order, it is the middle number. For an even number of data arranged in order, it is the number halfway between the two middle numbers.

Meniscus (URG Unit 16; SG Unit 16)
The curved surface formed when a liquid creeps up the side of a container (for example, a graduated cylinder).

Meter (m)
The standard unit of length measure in the metric system. One meter is approximately 39 inches.

Milliliter (ml) (URG Unit 16; SG Unit 16)
A measure of capacity in the metric system that is the volume of a cube that is one centimeter long on each edge.

Multiple (URG Unit 3 & Unit 11)
A number is a multiple of another number if it is evenly divisible by that number. For example, 12 is a multiple of 2 since 2 divides 12 evenly.

N

Numerator (URG Unit 13)
The number written above the line in a fraction. For example, the 2 is the numerator in the fraction $\frac{2}{5}$. (*See also* denominator.)

O

One-Dimensional Object (URG Unit 18; SG Unit 18)
An object is one-dimensional if it is made up of pieces of lines and curves.

Ordered Pairs (URG Unit 8)
A pair of numbers that gives the coordinates of a point on a grid in relation to the origin. The horizontal coordinate is given first; the vertical coordinate is given second. For example, the ordered pair (5, 3) tells us to move five units to the right of the origin and 3 units up.

Origin (URG Unit 8)
The point at which the *x*- and *y*-axes (horizontal and vertical axes) intersect on a coordinate plane. The origin is described by the ordered pair (0, 0) and serves as a reference point so that all the points on the plane can be located by ordered pairs.

P

Pack (URG Unit 4; SG Unit 4)
A cube that measures 10 cm on each edge. It is one of the base-ten pieces that is often used to represent 1000. (*See also* base-ten pieces.)

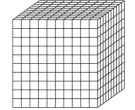

Palindrome (URG Unit 6)
A number, word, or phrase that reads the same forward and backward, e.g., 12321.

Parallel Lines (URG Unit 18)
Lines that are in the same direction. In the plane, parallel lines are lines that do not intersect.

Parallelogram (URG Unit 18)
A quadrilateral with two pairs of parallel sides.

Partitive Division (URG Unit 7)
Division as equal sharing. The total number of objects and the number of groups are known. The number of objects in each group is the unknown. For example, Frank has 144 marbles that he divides equally into 6 groups. How many marbles are in each group?

Pentagon (SG Unit 12)
A five-sided, five-angled polygon.

Perimeter (URG Unit 7; DAB Unit 7)
The distance around a two-dimensional shape.

Pint (URG Unit 16)
A unit of volume measure equal to 16 fluid ounces, i.e., two cups.

Polygon
A two-dimensional connected figure made of line segments in which each endpoint of every side meets with an endpoint of exactly one other side.

Population (URG Unit 1; SG Unit 1)
A collection of persons or things whose properties will be analyzed in a survey or experiment.

Prediction (SG Unit 1)
Using data to declare or foretell what is likely to occur.

Prime Number (URG Unit 11)
A number that has exactly two factors. For example, 7 has exactly two distinct factors, 1 and 7.

Prism
A three-dimensional figure that has two congruent faces, called bases, that are parallel to each other, and all other faces are parallelograms.

Prisms   Not a prism

Product (URG Unit 11; SG Unit 11; DAB Unit 11)
The answer to a multiplication problem. In the problem $3 \times 4 = 12$, 12 is the product.

Q

Quadrilateral (URG Unit 18)
A polygon with four sides.

Quart (URG Unit 16)
A unit of volume equal to 32 fluid ounces; one quarter of a gallon.

R

Recording Sheet (URG Unit 4)
A place value chart used for addition and subtraction problems.

Rectangular Prism (URG Unit 18; SG Unit 18)
A prism whose bases are rectangles. A right rectangular prism is a prism having all faces rectangles.

Regular (URG Unit 7; DAB Unit 7)
A polygon is regular if all sides are of equal length and all angles are equal.

Remainder (URG Unit 7)
Something that remains or is left after a division problem. The portion of the dividend that is not evenly divisible by the divisor, e.g., $16 \div 5 = 3$ with 1 as a remainder.

Right Angle (SG Unit 12)
An angle that measures 90°.

Rotation (turn) (URG Unit 12)
A transformation (motion) in which a figure is turned a specified angle and direction around a point.

Row (URG Unit 11)
In an array, the objects lined up horizontally.

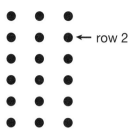

← row 2

Rubric (URG Unit 2)
A written guideline for assigning scores to student work, for the purpose of assessment.

S

Sample (URG Unit 1; SG Unit 1)
A part or subset of a population.

Skinny (URG Unit 4; SG Unit 4)
A block that measures 1 cm × 1 cm × 10 cm. It is one of the base-ten pieces that is often used to represent 10. (*See also* base-ten pieces.)

Square Centimeter (sq cm) (SG Unit 5)
The area of a square that is 1 cm long on each side.

Square Number (SG Unit 11)
A number that is the product of a whole number multiplied by itself. For example, 25 is a square number since $5 \times 5 = 25$. A square number can be represented by a square array with the same number of rows as columns. A square array for 25 has 5 rows of 5 objects in each row or 25 total objects.

Standard Masses
A set of objects with convenient masses, usually 1 g, 10 g, 100 g, etc.

Sum (URG Unit 2; SG Unit 2)
The answer to an addition problem.

Survey (URG Unit 14; SG Unit 14)
An investigation conducted by collecting data from a sample of a population and then analyzing it. Usually surveys are used to make predictions about the entire population.

T

Tangrams (SG Unit 12)
A type of geometric puzzle. A shape is given and it must be covered exactly with seven standard shapes called tans.

Thinking Addition (URG Unit 2)
A strategy for subtraction that uses a related addition problem. For example, $15 - 7 = 8$ because $8 + 7 = 15$.

Three-Dimensional (URG Unit 18; SG Unit 18)
Existing in three-dimensional space; having length, width, and depth.

TIMS Laboratory Method (URG Unit 1; SG Unit 1)
A method that students use to organize experiments and investigations. It involves four components: draw, collect, graph, and explore. It is a way to help students learn about the scientific method.

Turn (URG Unit 12)
(*See* rotation.)

Turn-Around Facts (URG Unit 2 & Unit 11 p. 37; SG Unit 11)
Addition facts that have the same addends but in a different order, e.g., $3 + 4 = 7$ and $4 + 3 = 7$. (*See also* commutative property of addition and commutative property of multiplication.)

Two-Dimensional (URG Unit 18; SG Unit 18)
Existing in the plane; having length and width.

Two-Pan Balance
A device for measuring the mass of an object by balancing the object against a number of standard masses (usually multiples of 1 unit, 10 units, and 100 units, etc.).

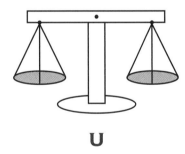

U

Unit (of measurement) (URG Unit 18)
A precisely fixed quantity used to measure. For example, centimeter, foot, kilogram, and quart are units of measurement.

Using a Ten (URG Unit 2)
1. A strategy for addition that uses partitions of the number 10. For example, one can find $8 + 6$ by thinking $8 + 6 = 8 + 2 + 4 = 10 + 4 = 14$.
2. A strategy for subtraction that uses facts that involve subtracting 10. For example, students can use $17 - 10 = 7$ to learn the "close fact" $17 - 9 = 8$.

Using Doubles (URG Unit 2)
Strategies for addition and subtraction that use knowing doubles. For example, one can find $7 + 8$ by thinking $7 + 8 = 7 + 7 + 1 = 14 + 1 = 15$. Knowing $7 + 7 = 14$ can be helpful in finding $14 - 7 = 7$ and $14 - 8 = 6$.

V

Value (URG Unit 1; SG Unit 1)
The possible outcomes of a variable. For example, red, green, and blue are possible values for the variable *color*. Two meters and 1.65 meters are possible values for the variable *length*.

Variable (URG Unit 1; SG Unit 1)
1. An attribute or quantity that changes or varies.
2. A symbol that can stand for a variable.

Vertex (URG Unit 12; SG Unit 12)
1. A point where the sides of a polygon meet.
2. A point where the edges of a three-dimensional object meet.

Vertical Axis (SG Unit 1)
In a coordinate grid, the *y*-axis. It is perpendicular to the horizontal axis.

Volume (URG Unit 16; SG Unit 16)
The measure of the amount of space occupied by an object.

Volume by Displacement (URG Unit 16)
A way of measuring volume of an object by measuring the amount of water (or some other fluid) it displaces.

W

Weight (URG Unit 9)
A measure of the pull of gravity on an object. One unit for measuring weight is the pound.

X

Y

Z